FAMILY WALKS
AROUND BRISTOL, BATH
AND THE MENDIPS

Nigel Vile

HIGH INTEREST · LOW MILEAGE

Scarthin Books, Cromford, Derbyshire

A

i

FAMILY WALKS
AROUND BRISTOL, BATH
AND THE MENDIPS

Family Walks Series
General Editor: Norman Taylor

————

THE COUNTRY CODE
Enjoy the countryside and respect its life and work
Guard against all risk of fire
Fasten all gates
Keep your dogs under proper control
Keep to public paths across farmland
Use gates and stiles to cross fences, hedges and walls
Leave livestock, crops and machinery alone
Take your litter home
Help to keep all water clean
Protect wildlife, plants and trees
Take special care on country roads
Make no unnecessary noise

————

Published by Scarthin Books, Cromford, Derbyshire, 1987
Reprinted 1989. Revised 1990. Reprinted 1993. Reprinted 1995.

Phototypesetting, printing by Higham Press Ltd., Shirland, Derbyshire

ISBN 0 907758 36 3

THE WESTBURY WHITE HORSE

1

Preface

There is surely no better way of appreciating our environment, both the natural and the man-made, than by walking. Away from the hustle-and-bustle of our towns, cities and main roads lie footpaths and tracks, hamlets and villages, which time seems to have passed by and which are crying out to be explored! Such beauty and tranquility simply cannot be appreciated from a motor-vehicle. The car-windscreen provides merely a goldfish-bowl view of the world with no opportunity to linger and absorb the atmosphere of the great outdoors. I am reminded of the couple that I met some years ago in a coffee-shop in Kent. The previous day, they had 'done' Cornwall to East Sussex, taking in en-route Exeter Cathedral, Corfe Castle, Winchester Cathedral and Arundel Castle. I could fully understand the wife's frustrations! With these thoughts in mind, I commend these walks to you as a gentle introduction to some of the countryside around two of England's most famous and historic cities.

Acknowledgements

I would like to thank Juliet Greaves of Bradford-on-Avon for the marvellous sketches which illustrate some of the walks. Thanks are also due to my wife, Gill, and our daughters Laura and Katie, all of whom accompanied me on a number of trial runs.

About the Author

A Bristolian by birth, Nigel Vile has lived and worked in the Bath and Bristol area for much of his life. Whilst teaching Economics and Environmental Studies at Corsham near Bath, he has attempted to interest youngsters in their surroundings on field-study visits to the Wiltshire Downlands and the Mendips. Married with three children, he lives in the picturesque town of Bradford-on-Avon some eight miles from Bath.

CONTENTS

MAP OF THE AREA

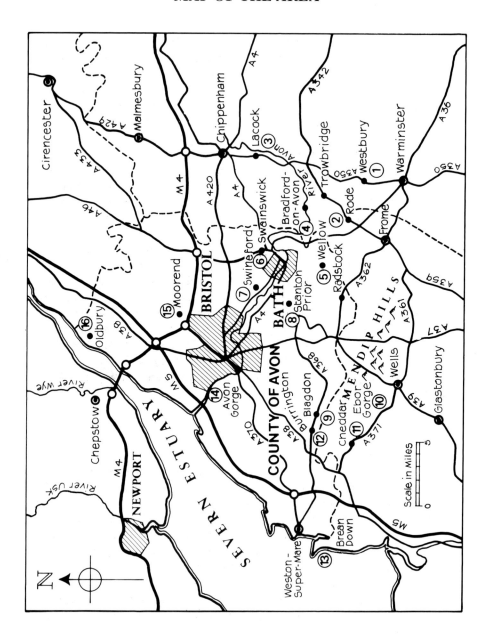

INTRODUCTION

The focus of this book is upon "Family Walks". Do not expect Herculean treks of Wainwright or Poucher dimensions. The objective is to provide relatively short and undemanding walks with a variety of attractions to stimulate the interest of youngsters. It may be the ever-popular stream or river, a long barrow or a White Horse, or some interesting wildlife. It is vitally important to develop in our youngsters an interest in outdoor pursuits such as rambling. As I write this, in front of me lies a newspaper article describing the vast amounts of time that many children spend in front of the television screen. Life is too often experienced second-hand. The perfect antidote to this is a country ramble where human settlements and wildlife habitats can be explored and experienced first-hand.

The area around Bath and Bristol is tremendously rich and varied. To the west lies the Severn Estuary, a unique environment explored in the walks centred upon Brean Down and Oldbury. To the south lies the limestone upland of the Mendip Hills with their dramatic gorges. In the east we can follow the Avon Valley as it passes between Bath and the Saxon town of Bradford-on-Avon, and beyond, around 'the National Trust village of Lacock. Farther on lie the chalk uplands of the Wiltshire Downs featured in the walk around the Westbury White Horse. Just north of Bath we touch the southern end of the Cotswold Hills, introduced in the walk around Swainswick.

Choosing a walk
Unless the children taking part in the walk are experienced walkers it is advisable to choose one or two of the easier walks first. Uneven field paths and muddy tracks are far harder going than the pavements or neatly-cut Park grass with which youngsters are most familiar. Routes 2, 3, 5 and 15 make ideal introductory half-day rambles. On more difficult routes a good idea is to make contingency plans so that if the party gets part-way, and the little ones are in danger of being put off walking for life, rescue can be arranged by meeting friends with transport at a suitable point, or by a driver in the party hurrying back to collect the car. At the back of the book I have made a personal assessment of the routes in order of difficulty.

Allowing sufficient time.

Each walk is intended to take up the best part of a half or whole day, allowing time for play, exploration and rest stops. It is better to over-estimate rather than under-estimate the time required, thus avoiding the need to have to 'route march' the latter part of the journey. As a rough guide, allow a pace of around one mile per hour for very young children, graduating to two miles per hour for the experienced ten-year-old.

What to wear.

It should go without saying that, given the British climate, it is advisable to go walking prepared for the worst! Proper walking-boots or stout shoes are preferable to wellington boots, which are fine for walking the dog in the park but are tiring and rub on more serious walks. On top, I prefer several thin layers that can gradually be peeled off as it gets warmer, rather than one thick jumper that just gives the hot/cold options! Waterproof cagoules are a must, too. Cords are better than jeans, the latter being extremely uncomfortable when wet due to their 'clinginess'. A cap or bobble-hat is also quite useful, bearing in mind that the crown of the head is where the body's greatest heat-loss will occur. Don't forget a small rucksack for all those items that seem to be needed on a walk - picnics, surplus clothing, maps, cameras and so on.

Route-finding.

The maps in this book, taken in conjunction with the directions supplied, should prove more than adequate when it comes to route finding. For those who like to carry O.S. maps when out walking, the sheets 172, 173, 182 and 183 cover all of the walks described in this book, with sheet 172 'Bristol and Bath' being especially useful.

Refreshments.

I have indicated where public-houses, cafes and tea-rooms can be found on the walks. Most of the pubs en route allow children accompanied by adults on to their premises.

Teashop opening times vary according to the time of year and expected custom, but most can be relied upon to stay open until five or six o'clock during the summer months. Where no refreshment stops are found on the route itself, I have suggested suitable picnic spots or convenient hostelries in the immediate area.

Conclusion.

Do not forget the Country Code. It should go without saying that all gates should be closed, that no litter should be dropped, that public paths should be kept to and that walls and hedgerows should not be damaged. Ramblers need the farmer as their friend, not their enemy, and it is our duty to cultivate a responsible attitude towards the countryside both in our children and ourselves. Finally, I wish you as much pleasure in walking these routes as I had in preparing them!

FORD AT WELLOW (Route 5)

Symbols used on the route maps

road

settlement

path or track

river

Church with spire

Church with tower

trees

bridge or aqueduct

canal

Antiquity

parking

triangulation pillar

building

number corresponding with route directions

Westbury and the White Horse

Outline   A circular perambulation based upon the Westbury White Horse.

Summary   Wiltshire is renowned for her chalk hill-figures, and this walk is centred on the famous White Horse carved into the hillside above Westbury. The route follows the edge of the downland escarpment, and the flat downland hill-tops. The paths are flat and gentle, but are exposed and windswept and offer little protection in terms of tree cover for the walker. Given this, and the far-ranging views, a clear fine day should be picked for the walk.

Attractions   Throughout this walk, the conflict between economic and social development on the one hand, and the need for conservation on the other, are evident. There are many fine points of interest on the route - hill-top paths, glorious views, traditional downland, an iron-age camp and a fine hill-figure - but equally there are the imprints of modern man - a cement works, a chalk quarry that supplies the works, Ministry of Defence land to which the public is denied access and a real 'honey-pot' tourist trap in the form of the White Horse which is all too often grossly over-crowded. It is vital that our children develop an awareness of these pressures and conflicts that come upon the natural environment.

The first section of the walk sees the path following the top of the scarp slope. The views are truly extensive. On a clear day, they encompass the Mendips, the Cotswolds, the Welsh Mountains and the Marlborough Downs, as well as many local towns and villages. The topograph near the White Horse details exact places and distances. Totally dominating the view with its massive chimney is the Blue Circle Cement Works, located at Westbury due to the presence of two vital raw materials - chalk and clay.

On the right-hand side of the track leading to the Ministry of Defence Post, lies a vast chalk quarry, from where slurried chalk is pumped to the cement works. The quarry has been carefully concealed behind trees and hedgerows, and with the pipeline obviating the need for a fleet of heavy lorries, the workings are far less obtrusive than the actual cement works!

continued on page 12

Route 1

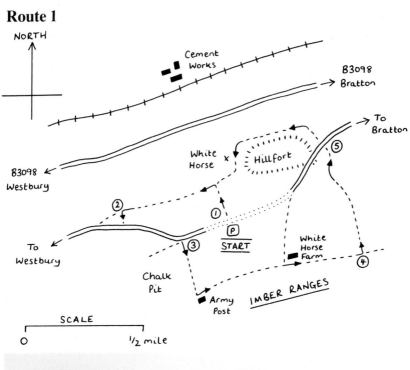

NORTH

Cement Works

B3098 Bratton

To Bratton

B3098 Westbury

White Horse × Hillfort

⑤

② ①

To Westbury

③ Ⓟ START

White Horse Farm

④

Chalk Pit

Army Post

IMBER RANGES

SCALE

0   ½ mile

BLUE CIRCLE CEMENT WORKS

10

Route 1

Westbury and the White Horse 2½ miles

START *From the Town Square in Westbury, take the minor road that is signposted to the 'White Horse'. It is a two-mile drive to the top of the Downs where a vast grassed area is available for parking. (G.R. 899514)*

ROUTE

1. *Walk across to the hill-fort and turn left, passing the topograph. Continue along the hill-top path, following the path beside the wire fence on the edge of the hill.*

2. *At the small wood, bear left and look for a stile at the top of the field. Climb the stile out on to the road, and turn left. After walking a short distance along the road, you reach a cross-roads - the road bears left and a chalk-track goes straight ahead.*

3. *Continue along this chalk track to an army check-point. Turn left, and follow the path that borders the northern perimeter of Imber Ranges. Continue along this path, past White Horse Farm, as far as the next path on the left which is an enclosed track reached through a gate.*

4. *Follow this track on to open ground, and then continue along a sunken path which is followed through to the Bratton to Westbury White Horse road.*

5. *Cross the road and climb up on to the ramparts of the hill-fort, and follow these ancient embankments around to the White Horse itself. The views from here are far-ranging. It is then but a short walk back to the car-park.*

Public Transport Westbury is served by trains from both Bath and Bristol, but the station is a couple of miles from this particular walk. A local Westbury to Bratton bus-service passes the foot of the White Horse.

The path from the Ministry of Defence Post past White Horse Farm borders the vast Imber Ranges on Salisbury Plain. This huge tract of land is closed to the public, and signs appear with alarming regularity warning of danger of unexploded shells! Several miles across the Plain lies the deserted village of Imber, where in 1943 the villagers were given just six weeks notice to quit before the Army moved in to utilise the site for urban warfare training. Paradoxically, the Army's occupation of the Plain has preserved it from over-development, as can be seen on the few days during each year when the roads across to Imber are open for public use.

Bratton Castle, an iron-age hillfort, lies on the hilltop overlooking the flat clay-vale beneath. The double-bank and ditch of the Castle's southern perimeter are in good repair, and if you scramble up these ramparts you will find a 25 acre enclosure containing a long-barrow. Alongside the fort lies the White Horse. The original horse, said to have commemorated King Alfred's victory over the Danes in the 9th century was a cart-horse! In 1778, it was 'remodelled' by a 'wretch named Gee' who was steward to Lord Abingdon. It is now 166 feet long and 163 feet in height, and is perhaps second only to the cement works' chimney when it comes to prominent local landmarks!

Kite-flying has always been a popular pastime with youngsters and adults alike. The large grassed area atop the Downs catches the wind well, too well on occasions, so whatever you do don't forget to bring a kite with you!

Refreshments There are none available on the route of the walk. However, it is difficult to find a more suitable picnic spot than on the Downs alongside the White Horse. Should you do this walk on a summer's weekend, you can guarantee an ice-cream van will be around somewhere! Nearby, Westbury has tea-rooms, public-houses and so on, and in Bratton, the Duke Hotel has a restaurant, bar food and a beer garden.

Route 2
2½ miles
Rode, Tellisford and the Somerset Frome

Outline Rode ~ Tellisford ~ Rode.

Summary A short walk that follows level lanes and field-paths on either side of a one-mile stretch of the Frome. This river, a tributary of the Bristol Avon, has its source a few miles to the south of the Somerset town of the same name. On its fifteen-mile journey to join the Avon at Freshford, near Bath, its course passes through several attractive villages on the Wiltshire - Somerset border, including the two visited on this walk.

Attractions The Frome is a quiet tributary of the Avon, and this walk follows a tranquil and idyllic section of its course. At both Rode and Tellisford, there are many attractive cottages, as well as long disused water-mills that were once part of the West of England woollen industry.

The riverside meadows between Langham Farm and Tellisford Bridge provide plenty of excellent picnicking spots, with the river immediately at hand for paddling or fishing for minnows. There is also a Second World War pill-box near to the weir at Tellisford, where imaginations can run riot! Tellisford Bridge provides a perfect location for a game of Pooh-sticks, or for gazing into the clear waters of the Frome to spot the trout and pike that swim up and down this section of river.

If all of this is not enough, then following the walk, no member of the family will fail to enjoy the delights of the Rode Tropical Bird Gardens, where a whole host of creatures ranging from penguins to owls, and from wallabies to rabbits are on display.

Refreshments There are public houses in Rode itself, and at the nearby Bird Gardens a full range of refreshments can be obtained. Although 'dry', Tellisford and its pleasant riverside meadows provides the walker with excellent picnic spots.

Route 2

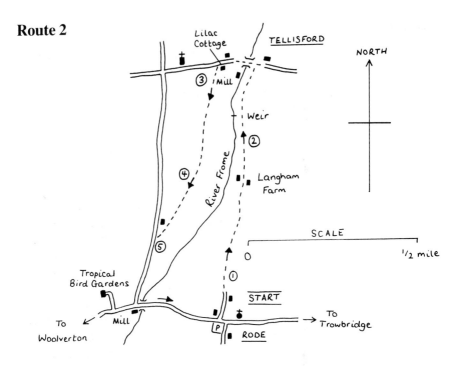

LANGHAM FARM

Route 2
Rode, Tellisford and the Somerset Frome   2½ miles

START   *Although lying just off the major roads in the area, the village of Rode is easy to find. The map shows where the village lies in relation to the local road network. Ample parking will be found on the village streets.* (G.R. 805542)

ROUTE

1. *The route to Langham Farm is to be found at the northern end of the village. A little way down the hill from the church, a lane occasionally sign-posted 'Slalom Site' indicates the start of the walk. At first, this lane is a tarmac path, but shortly it turns into a rough track. The river is in the valley on the left, and Tellisford Church can be seen on the hill away in the distance. Take the path to the right of the buildings at Langham Farm, and climb the gate into the riverside meadow.*

2. *Follow the river bank to a stile, and from there continue along the riverside path. A weir will very shortly appear on the left. On reaching Tellisford Bridge, cross the river and climb the hill through the village, passing several picturesque cottages. Just past the last cottage on the left, Lilac Cottage, climb the gate into the field.*

3. *The right-of-way, although not way-marked, crosses this field. Keep to the hill-top, with the river below on your left. Scenic views of the earlier part of the walk are had from this side of the river. Continue past the right-hand side of the clump of trees ahead.*

4. *The right-of-way continues unmarked across open-fields. You must keep your eyes open for the bungalow ahead that indicates the site of Rocks Farm. Aim straight for the bungalow, taking a detour around the edge of the fields should crops be growing. Pass to the left of the bungalow, out on to the lane.*

5. *Turn left and follow this lane on to a junction. Turn left, passing the now disused Rode Mill, cross Rode Bridge, and head back up the road to retrace your steps back to the start of the walk.*

Public Transport   The Bath to Warminster bus-service stops at the Memorial Hall in Rode. This is approximately a two-hourly service, and therefore the actual times should be checked with Badgerline, the operators.

THE FORD THROUGH BIDE BROOK

16

Lacock and Reybridge

Outline Lacock ~ Reybridge ~ Lacock.

Summary A short and gentle walk alongside the River Avon, in and around the picture-postcard village of Lacock. The National Trust owns and manages the greater part of the village, and consequently there are few concessions to the 20th century.

Attractions The village of Lacock is undoubtedly the main attraction on this particular walk. The settlement dates back to Saxon times, if not earlier, and has been described as 'easily the most remarkable and the most beautiful in Wiltshire'. The village is based around four streets - Church Street, West and East Streets and the High Street - and still very much resembles a medieval town. Lacock's attractive houses cover every century from the thirteenth to the eighteenth, with little more recent development to spoil the overall effect. The whole is admirably overseen and managed by the National Trust, with even the telephone box being an unobtrusive shade of grey! There is so much to see in Lacock - its Abbey, the Fox Talbot Museum of Photography, St Cyriac's Church, the tithe barn, the village cross, the pack-horse bridge, and so on - that the interested visitor should purchase a copy of the Trust's guide to Lacock from their shop in the High Street.

The Bristol Avon between Lacock and Reybridge meanders across a flat clay vale that, in the days before flood relief schemes and sluice gates, would have been frequently under water. This is evident from the raised causeways at both Reybridge and Lacock. An assortment of flora and fauna have their habitat along this section of the river - it should not be difficult in the summer months to spot dragon-flies, water lilies, teazles and moorhen along the course of the river, with timid rabbits feeding alongside in the riverside meadows.

The tarmac path back across the fields from Reybridge to Lacock is sited slightly above the level of the river, giving wide views to the east. Immediately at hand is the Avon, beyond which - and several hundred feet higher - lies Naish and Bowden Hills, rising to a height of 589 feet above sea level (the Avon here is just 150 feet above sea level). The more gentle slopes of this higher land are given over to arable farming, with woodland emerging on the higher slopes.

Route 3

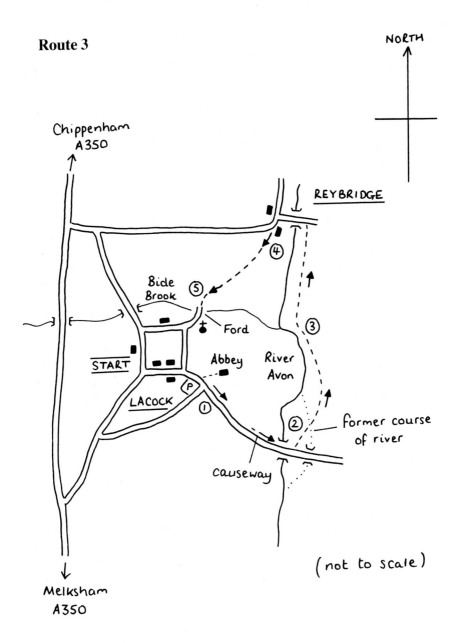

NORTH

Chippenham
A350

REYBRIDGE

④

Bide
Brook   ⑤

Ford

③

START

Abbey   River
Avon

LACOCK   Ⓟ

①   ②   former course
of river

causeway

(not to scale)

Melksham
A350

Route 3
Lacock and Reybridge

2½ miles

START   *Lacock lies just half-a-mile off the main A350 Chippenham to Melksham Road. At the far end of the High Street, opposite the entrance to Lacock Abbey and the Fox Talbot Museum, is a free car-park. (G.R. 917684)*

ROUTE

1. *Turn right along the road on leaving the car-park, heading out into the countryside and away from the village. Use the pavement alongside the sometimes rather busy Devizes Road, that follows the southern boundary wall of the Abbey Grounds. After a few hundred yards, a causeway carries the path over the Avon's flood-plain, before a stone bridge crosses the river itself. As there is no pavement on the bridge, extreme care needs to be taken. Look out for a stile in the left-hand wall, which is crossed into the adjoining field.*

2. *Bear right, across the first field. Aim for the telegraph-pole by the opposite hedge, next to which is a stile. Head straight across the next, much smaller, field to a gate in the opposite hedgerow, and in the third field head straight across towards another telegraph pole, next to which is a gate. Once across this gate, the River Avon comes into view a few yards below.*

3. *Keeping the Avon on your left, follow the river-side path all of the way through to Reybridge, where a stile is crossed on to the road. Turn left, crossing the river on an attractive stone bridge. A row of pretty thatched cottages will immediately face you, at the road junction at the far side of the bridge. Here you should turn left.*

4. *Pass between the pair of cottages, on the bend where the road bears to the right. Follow the tarmac path through a gate and across the fields back towards Lacock. At the far end of the path, turn left down the lane, and continue on into Lacock. Cross Bide Brook on the pack-horse bridge next to the ford.*

5. *Returning to Lacock, turn right into Church Street, and then first left into East Street. This leads through to the High Street and the car-park, although most visitors will now wish to explore the delights of Lacock village, or visit one of the many tea-rooms or inns!*

Public Transport Badgerline, the Country fleet name of Bristol Omnibus, operate an hourly service from Trowbridge to Chippenham, via Melksham, that stops outside the Red Lion in Lacock. Both Trowbridge and Chippenham have bus and rail links with Bath and Bristol.

Refreshments In Lacock, teas can be obtained from King John's Hunting Lodge or the Stable Tea Rooms. There are three attractive inns - the Red Lion, the George, and the Carpenter's Arms. There is also the Sign of the Angel Hotel. There are no refreshment facilities at Reybridge, although the river bank between Lacock and this much smaller settlement provides ideal spots for picnics.

THE KENNET AND AVON CANAL

The Kennet and Avon Canal

Outline   Dundas ~ Conkwell ~ Winsley ~ Avoncliff ~ Dundas.

Summary   Between Bradford-on-Avon and Bath, the Bristol Avon flows through the beautiful Limpley Stoke Valley. In addition to the river, the valley also carries the Kennet and Avon Canal, the Bristol to Southampton railway, and the A36 trunk road to the south coast. From Dundas, with its famous aqueduct carrying the canal over the Avon, a steep climb is necessary to reach the hamlet of Conkwell, high above the valley. From Conkwell, lanes and field paths are followed to Winsley, where a path drops down to the valley bottom at Avoncliff. From here, a two-mile towpath walk along the recently restored Kennet and Avon Canal returns the walker to Dundas.

Attractions   Dundas is the site of perhaps the finest aqueduct in the south of England. It is also the junction of the Kennet and Avon Canal with the long-disused Somerset Coal Canal, a link that necessitated the construction of a substantial wharf, where today pleasure-craft of many shapes and sizes are moored. The first quarter-of-a-mile of the Coal Canal has recently been restored to provide additional moorings.

The climb to Conkwell, high above the canal, provides excellent views along the Avon valley towards the outskirts of Bath. Conkwell itself is a small hamlet of stone-built cottages, once the homes of local quarrymen and their families employed extracting the famous local stone. The stone was carried down the hill-side on a tramline to the canal below, before being transported into Bath where it was used as building material.

The quiet and level stretch of the walk to Winsley, through fine open countryside, provides extensive views away towards the Marlborough Downs in the east, and the Westbury Hills to the south. Both the Cherhill and Westbury White Horses should be visible on a clear day. From Winsley, another village of attractive stone cottages, the path down the hillside to Avoncliff provides one of the most panoramic views of the West Wiltshire countryside available in the area. Immediately at hand is the Avon Valley with, to the left, Bradford-on-Avon and its terraces of stone cottages tumbling down the hillside. Beyond, the scarp slopes of some of Wiltshire's Downland may be seen, with particular landmarks

continued on page 24

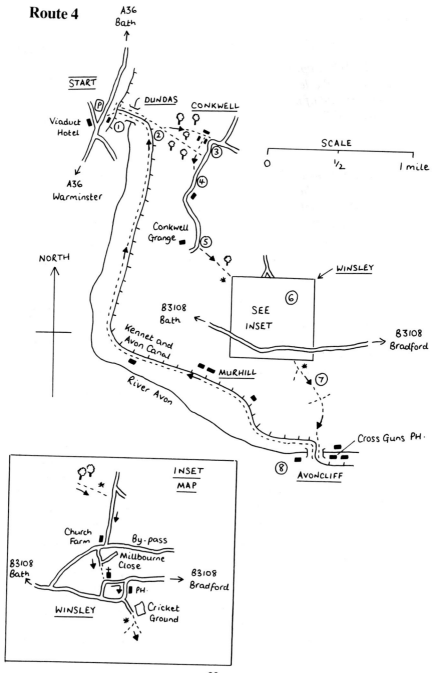

Route 4

A36
Bath

START

DUNDAS   CONKWELL

Viaduct
Hotel

① ② ③ ④ ⑤

A36
Warminster

SCALE

0   ½   1 mile

Conkwell
Grange

NORTH

WINSLEY

B3108
Bath

SEE
INSET

⑥

B3108
Bradford

Kennet and
Avon Canal

MURHILL

⑦

River Avon

Cross Guns PH.

⑧   AVONCLIFF

INSET
MAP

Church
Farm   By-pass

Millbourne
Close

B3108
Bath

B3108
Bradford

PH.

WINSLEY

Cricket
Ground

22

Route 4

The Kennet and Avon Canal   5 miles

START *When approaching Dundas from Bath on the A36, there is a lay-by on the left just before the Monkton Combe Garage. At the southern end of the lay-by, a lane leads down to the Kennet and Avon Canal and Dundas Aqueduct. The A36 is a busy-road, so extreme care is necessary.* (G.R. 783625)

ROUTE

1. *From the crane by the Wharf, take the footbridge on your left across to the far side of the canal. Cross the aqueduct, and at the end of the path climb the stile into Conkwell Woods.*

2. *Rather than climbing straight up the hillside on what is the bed of the old mineral tramway, bear left into an open field. Head diagonally across the field, taking in the open views of the Avon Valley, until a stile is reached. Follow the path as it borders the edge of the woodland up the hillside into Conkwell.*

3. *The first cottage on your right is named 'Spring Cottage'. Bear right immediately past the cottage, on to a way-marked path. Follow this path through deciduous woodland for about half-a-mile, before joining a quiet country lane. Avoid any right turns, especially the one that returns you to Dundas rather prematurely!*

4. *Turn right along this lane, which is followed for about half-a-mile through open-countryside. On a clear day, the Marlborough Downs will be visible away to the east.*

5. *At a bend in the road, near to Conkwell Grange, a stile on your left takes you into open fields. The right-of-way is unfortunately not sign-posted. Cross the first field, aiming for the right of the clump of trees ahead. Follow the right-hand boundary of the second field, out on to the lane beyond. Turn right, and head towards Church Farm and Winsley.*

6. *The route through Winsley is shown on the inset map. The three landmarks that you should pass are firstly the Church, followed by the Seven Stars Public House and then the Cricket Club.*

7. *Follow the enclosed path down the hillside beyond the cricket ground, avoiding the right-hand fork. It is on this down-hill path that the excellent view noted earlier is obtained. Pass through the kissing-gate at the bottom of the path, cross the track ahead, and take the public right-of-way diagonally across the open-field ahead, down the hill to Avoncliff.*

8. *From Avoncliff, the two-mile return journey to Dundas is quite simply the canal tow-path. Make sure that you follow the way-marked route to Limpley Stoke, by taking the path under the aqueduct to reach the opposite towpath.*

––––––––––

being Roundway Hill above Devizes, and Cley Hill alongside Warminster. There is also no escaping the ever-present Westbury White Horse.

At Avoncliff there is much to admire. Another aqueduct that carries the canal over the Avon, a weir, disused water-mills, stone cottages and an excellent pub - the Cross Guns - where a refreshing pint can be enjoyed on a terraced garden that fronts the river. Afternoon teas are also available in a nearby cottage.

The two-mile towpath walk back to Dundas is canal-walking at its best. The canal clings to the valley side, slightly above the River Avon, overhung by trees on both banks. The waterway is a haven for wildlife, with ducks and moorhens being the easiest species to spot. Just by the Winsley Hill bridge, there is a tea-garden in a canal-side cottage where welcome refreshments can be obtained near to the end of what is one of my favourite rambles.

Footnote   The Kennet and Avon Canal connects the Avon at Bath with the Thames at Reading, thus providing a London to Bristol waterway. The Kennet in the name comes from the fact that the Newbury to Reading section of the canal makes frequent use of this particular river. Completed in 1810, the main cargo carried along the waterway was Somerset Coal, brought through to the canal at Dundas from the mining centre of Radstock via the Somerset Coal Canal. After many years of decay and neglect, the Kennet and Avon is being restored, with much of its length in Wiltshire now navigable.

Refreshments   Viaduct Hotel, Dundas. Seven Stars, Winsley. Cross Guns and tea-shop at Avoncliff. Tea-garden on canal near Winsley Hill bridge.

Wellow and Stony Littleton Long Barrow

Outline   Wellow ~ Wellow Ford ~ Stony Littleton Long Barrow ~ Wellow Brook ~ Wellow.

Summary   A hillside village, a ford, a hill-top path, a long barrow, and a riverside path, all in a peaceful countryside which is strangely so close to the City of Bath. The walk has just one or two short steep sections - the climb down to Wellow Brook from Wellow at the start, and the return at journey's end - but in the main it is level bridleway, field path and quiet country lane.

Attractions   Wellow is best approached from Hinton Charterhouse. The village, with its southerly aspect, can be seen in the distance clinging to the hillside, with Wellow Brook flowing along in the valley below. Ultimately, it will join the Bristol Avon near Monkton Combe.

Wellow contains many attractive cottages, centred on the village square and the 'Fox and Badger' public house. At the eastern end of the village, just off this particular walk but nonetheless worth a visit, lies the village church of St. Julian, standing aloft above a rolling landscape of hills, valleys and fields.

Wellow Brook is crossed initially by a foot-bridge, alongside which the stream has been forded. Following heavy rain, the road can be under several inches of water, as is evident from the measuring pole alongside the ford - it is capable of measuring depths of up to six feet above the road level!

The bridleway leading towards Stony Littleton Long Barrow provides a perfect opportunity to see at first-hand typical English hedgerows and verges. In Spring and Summer, the path is awash with a vast array of flora, ranging from red campion and the dog rose, to comfrey and self-heal. It is well worth carrying a pocket-guide to help identify the many varieties or, better still, to equip your youngsters with an I-Spy Wild Flowers book!

From the bridleway, a fine view of the locality is obtained, taking in the Brook in the valley below, the village of Wellow on the opposite hillside, St. Julian's Church prominent at the eastern end of the village, and - if your eye-sight is very sharp - the course of the old Somerset and Dorset Railway. This 71 mile line ran from Bath to Bournemouth, and

continued on page 28

25

Route 5

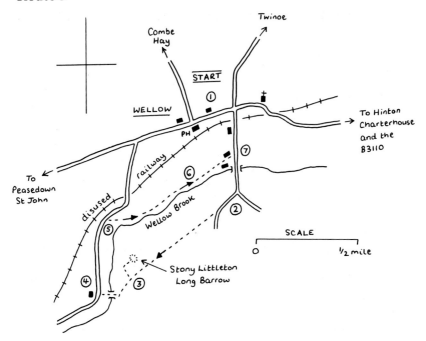

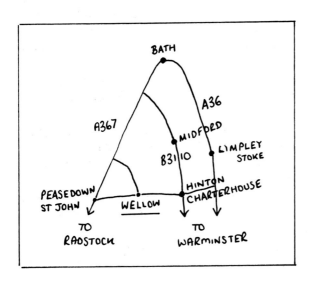

Route 5

Wellow and Stony Littleton Long Barrow   2½ miles

START   *The road to Wellow from Hinton Charterhouse passes under a viaduct that carried the Somerset and Dorset Railway, before climbing up into the village itself. St. Julian's Church is passed on the right, before the road enters the village square. There is ample room for parking on the road in the vicinity of the Fox and Badger Public House.* (G.R. 741583)

ROUTE

1. *Walk back towards the church, taking the first turning on the right that leads down to Wellow Brook and the ford. Cross the river, by either the ford or the foot-bridge, depending on the water level!*

2. *Continue along the lane for a short distance, bear right at the fork and look for a sign-posted bridleway on the right-hand side. Follow this bridleway for half-a-mile, then cross a gate and continue along an obvious field path. The Long Barrow will soon be visible on the right, but avoid the temptation of simply crossing the field at this point, where there is no right-of-way, to reach the tumulus.*

3. *Continue along the path until a sign points the way to the Long Barrow. Follow the signs to the site, where you will undoubtedly spend time exploring, before retracing your steps back to the main path. Continue down the hill, cross the footbridge over Wellow Brook, and emerge on to the quiet Wellow to Shoscombe Lane opposite a cottage named 'Greenacres'.*

4. *Turn right along this lane, back in the direction of Wellow. Follow this quiet lane for approximately half-a-mile, with the Brook over the hedgerow on the right.*

5. *A gate and a stile in the hedgerow on the right will take you into the fields that border Wellow Brook. Either follow the official path across the fields back towards Wellow, or follow the unofficial but most-popular path that immediately borders the river!*

6. *Where the path seemingly ends, and the river bears off to the right, there is a stile in the hedgerow to your left. The path then passes through one or two small enclosures back towards Wellow.*

7. *The path then passes by some cottages, and emerges on a lane a little way up from the ford. It is but a few minutes walk up the hill to the village.*

27

---

survived for just over a century from its opening in 1862 to its closure courtesy of Dr. Beeching in 1966. The line held legendary status amongst railway enthusiasts, passing as it did through some of the best scenery in Southern England. The old 'S-and-D' - 'serene and delightful' to its many friends, but 'slow and dirty' to its critics - may be long gone, but I am sure that the ghost of the old Pines Express taking its weekly load of tourists from the north country to the South Coast still haunts these hillsides!

Stony Littleton Long Barrow is a Neolithic Tomb used for collective burial and dating back to 2000 BC. A plaque at its entrance boasts that 'this tumulus is declared by competent judges to be the most perfect specimen of Celtic Antiquity still existing in Great Britain' - it is hard to disagree. It evidently became 'much injured' due to 'the lapse of time or the carelessness of its former proprietors' but was 'restored in 1858 with scrupulous exactness'. It is possible to enter the barrow to a depth of 50 feet from the entrance and to examine the three pairs of burial chambers that lie on either side of the central gallery. It is advisable to carry a torch on this particular walk for this purpose.

The final section of the walk back to the village follows the peaceful meadows that border Wellow Brook. The Brook at this point meanders on its way to join the Bristol Avon. On the outside bend of each meander, where the full force of the water and its erosive power are felt, deep pools of water have been formed as both the river bank and bed are worn away. This contrasts with the inside bends, where the slower moving water deposits its bed-load to form shallows. The flora along the river bank is once again rich and varied. Close-by, the clear waters of the Brook should make it possible to spot the trout that are synonymous with the Avon tributaries south of Bath. The river bank and its environment provides a perfect spot for a picnic, before the ascent back to Wellow and the end of the walk.

Refreshments   Fox and Badger, Wellow. Picnicking places on river bank.

Swainswick, Woolley and Langridge

Outline   Swainswick ~ Woolley ~ Landsdown ~ Langridge ~ Woolley ~ Swainswick.

Summary   A strenuous walk up and down steep valley sides north of Bath, taking in some magnificent rural landscapes.

Attractions   This walk passes through exhilarating countryside to the north of Bath, taking in valleys, hillsides, hill-tops, woodland and streams. The views are superb, and breath is therefore not the only thing that you will pause for! For example, just below Charlcombe Grove Farm this vista appears:

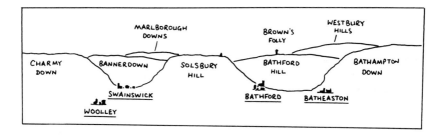

There are various flora and fauna to look out for, but I would encourage youngsters to put their energies into the walk and their inquisitiveness into simply appreciating the views and interpreting the landscape with, ideally, the aid of the 1:25000 series map covering Bath and Keynsham. This is an ideal environment for learning map-reading skills, with lengthy sections of the route being visible from the many viewpoints on the walk.

The hill-top at Landsdown was the site of a Civil War battle where the Royalist leader, Sir Bevil Grenville, was killed. A monument, just off of our route, was erected in 1720 to mark the spot where it is believed Sir Bevil fell (GR. 722703).

continued on page 32

29

Route 6

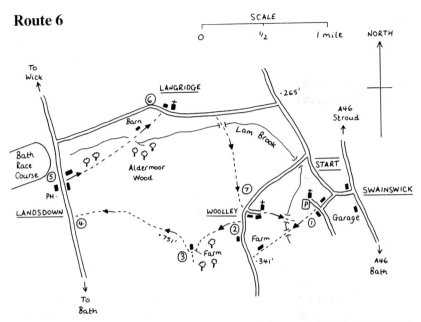

SCALE

0 1/2 1 mile

NORTH

To Wick

LANGRIDGE

·265'

A46 Stroud

Barn

Lam Brook

Bath Race Course

Aldermoor Wood

START

SWAINSWICK

PH·

LANDSDOWN

WOOLLEY

P

Garage

·751'

Farm

Farm

A46 Bath

Farm

·341'

To Bath

SOLSBURY HILL FROM CHARLECOMBE FARM

Route 6

Swainswick, Woolley and Langridge   4½ miles

(Variation 1 mile)

START   *Swainswick lies just off the A46 Bath to Stroud Road, two miles north of the junction with the A4 at Lambridge. There is room for sensible parking on the wide road just outside the Parish Church. (G.R. 756684).*

This walk has many excellent stiles with yellow way-marker arrows attached. Further, the wide-ranging views make it possible to gain an overview of large sections of the walk. For example, from the start it is possible to see the path down to Lam Brook, its continuation on past Crossleaze Farm to Woolley, its ascent on towards Charlcombe Farm and the flat hill-top of Landsdown.

ROUTE

1. *The Public Footpath sign points the way, through a cottage garden and down the field to a footbridge over Lam Brook in the valley bottom. Climb the field at the far side of the bridge, pass to the left of Crossleaze Farm, and then out on to the lane that leads to the village of Woolley. Turn right towards the village.*

2. *Just before the first house in the village, cross a gate into a field on your left, to continue the climb up towards Landsdown. A yellow marker should appear on a post by the gate. From here to Charlcombe Grove Farm, the path is indicated by yellow arrows that appear on the frequent stiles. At the first stile, the path bears left and then continues to do so all the way up to the farm.*

   (For the shorter walk, continue into Woolley, take the first road on the right to the village Church, and follow direction 7).

3. *Pass around the farm, and at the post indicating a crossing of paths, go straight across. Climb a short distance up the field in front, and then bear right to a stile in the wall ahead. A series of stiles and yellow arrows points the way on towards Landsdown, with each successive stile being clearly visible ahead as you cross the flat hill-top.*

4. *At the main road, turn right. You pass the Brathwayt Arms on your left, and a row of cottages on your right.*

5. *Immediately past the cottages, pass through a gateway on your right, and head straight down a track into a field. Aim for a gate in the wall ahead. A steep descent follows, through open fields with no apparent path! It is simply a case of passing straight down the hillside and keeping the river valley and the trees slightly to your left. An arrowed stile in a*

C   31

patch of woodland is crossed, and the descent then continues to the stream in the valley bottom. Cross a gate and the stream and continue up through two fields to the lane at Langridge. Keep a barn to your left, and Aldermoor Wood to your right.

6. *Turn right down the lane into Langridge. A little way past the Church, a stile is crossed into the fields on the right. Almost immediately, a footbridge crosses the stream on the left, and you pass into a field where the path heads diagonally to the top-corner. Arrowed stiles then bring you on to a well-defined path that follows the hillside to Woolley.*

7. *Go into the village, take the first left to the Church, and then follow the footpath to the right of 'All Saints'. Continue down the hillside to Lam Brook, cross the stream using a second footbridge (ie. not the one used at the outset), and walk a short distance along the opposite bank of the Brook before heading on up the hillside and returning to Swainswick.*

Public Transport   Bristol Omnibus operate an infrequent service from Bath to Tormarton via Swainswick.

The three hamlets on the walk possess Churches that are worth exploring. Langridge Church contains 16th century tombstones on the wall next to the altar, a 15th century brass commemorating the then Lord of the Manor's wife, Elizabeth Walshe, and a 14th century effigy of an unknown woman. Woolley Church was rebuilt in 1761 by John Wood the Younger. Its claim to fame is the grave of Admiral Peter Puget who, having sailed around the world with Captain Vancouver, was then immortalized in the name Puget Sound. He died in 1822. Swainswick Church contains the graves of both John Wood the Elder, and the aforementioned John Wood the Younger, the architects of Georgian Bath. After passing through the exceptional Norman doorway, look out for the brass of Edmund Forde, a former Lord of the Manor who died in 1439.

Refreshments   Half-way around the walk, and with the hardest climbing behind you, lies the Brathwayt Arms at Landsdown, on the main road by Bath race-course. Meals, bar-snacks and family garden.

Route 7

Swineford and the Bristol Avon

Outline Swineford ~ Upton Cheyney ~ Bitton ~ the Avon ~ Swineford.

Summary Pleasant walking on hillsides and river banks between Bath and Bristol. A gentle climb from Swineford to Upton Cheyney, a gradual descent to Bitton, and then level field paths, a disused railway line, and the river bank back to Swineford.

Attractions This walk passes through hard-working agricultural countryside between Bath and Bristol. When I walked the route during one August, there were two substantial herds of Friesian dairy-cows awaiting milking, acres of arable crops, especially maize and wheat, farmers busy hay-making and harvesting cereals, and young calves just lazing in the sunshine! At the right time of year, this is an excellent walk for observing the farming community hard at work, and seeing the many fruits of its labours!

Both Upton Cheyney and Bitton are commuter villages, with the majority of cottages having been bought up, renovated and restored by either Bath or Bristol business-people. The highlight in these villages is undoubtedly St. Mary's Church at Bitton, which is basically Norman, but where Roman brick-work and pavements have been found. The churchyard is full of old tomb-stones, and it is fascinating hunting around for those of greatest antiquity. See if you can beat one dated 1680!

The old railway track once formed part of the Midland Railway's Bristol Temple Meads to Bath Green Park line. Closed by Beeching in the 1960's, the local council have turned the old line into one of the country's first cycle/walkways. At the old Bitton Station, on the A431 just the Bristol-side of Bitton, the Bristol Suburban Railway Society have their base, with locomotives in steam several weekends each year. Being elevated above the surrounding countryside, the views from the old line are particularly good. On the right lies the Avon, surrounded by flat agricultural land, on the left the hills up above Bitton, with Upton Cheyney and North Stoke nestling on their slopes. Especially prominent is Kelston Round Hill, topped with its clump of trees.

The River Avon between Bath and Bristol is deep and navigable, and a steady stream of pleasure craft ply up and down these waters during

continued on page 36

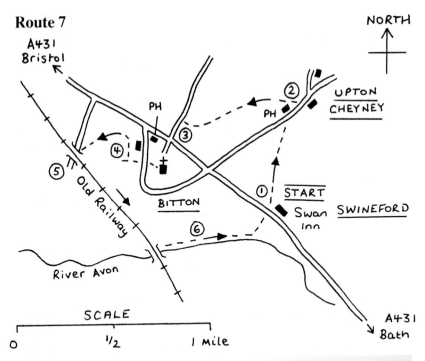

Route 7

A431
Bristol

NORTH

PH

PH

② UPTON
CHEYNEY

③

④

⑤ Old Railway

BITTON

① START
Swan
Inn

SWINEFORD

⑥

River Avon

A431
Bath

SCALE

0   ½   1 mile

THE AVON FROM THE CYCLEWAY BRIDGE

34

Route 7
Swineford and the Bristol Avon

3½ miles

START *Approaching Swineford from Bath along the busy A431 road, the Swan Inn is on the right-hand side. Just past the Swan, a right-turn is sign-posted to a picnic site. Park in this picnic area. As this walk uses part of a Kingswood District Council walk described in their leaflet 'Footpaths from Swineford', the route is generally well marked with clear paths and stiles. Details of the Council's walks are displayed in the car-park at the picnic site. (G.R. 690692).*

ROUTE

1. *Take the sign-posted footpath up the hillside towards Upton Cheyney. On reaching a road on the outskirts of the village, turn right and continue up the hill to the Upton Inn.*

2. *Just past the Inn, take the path on the left signposted 'Bitton'. Follow this path down through the fields to Bitton, obvious stiles way-marking the route.*

3. *The first buildings you pass in Bitton are local authority houses. The path past these homes then comes out on to a road - Golden Valley Lane - where you turn left and head down to the main A431 road. A slight detour to the right, along the pavement that borders the main road, brings you to the White Hart Inn and the village shop. Directly opposite Golden Valley Lane, across the main road, is Church Lane. Go down this lane, into Bitton Churchyard, and take the path to the right a short distance from the church itself.*

4. *This path brings you out on to a road, where you turn right past some cottages. Almost immediately, you take the public footpath sign-posted on the left. This crosses a stream, passes over a stile on the right-hand side, and then continues right around the perimeters of the fields until an old railway bridge is reached.*

5. *Scramble up one of the well-worn paths on to the old railway, which now forms the Bath to Bristol cycleway. The best way up is to pass under the bridge, and to take the scramble up on your left. It appears that some steps have actually been cut into the embankment at this point. Follow the old railway in a south-easterly direction, which means keeping the village of Bitton on your left.*

    Just before the railway crosses the Avon, take the steps down on the right-hand side to the river bank.

6. *Follow the path under the railway bridge, and along the river bank all the way back to Swineford and the picnic site.*

35

Public Transport Badgerline operate a regular Bath-Bristol service which passes through both Swineford and Bitton.

---

the summer months. It is equally popular with local anglers, with roach, chub, perch, gudgeon and eels being just some of its inhabitants. Many families of ducks also live along the river banks. The adjoining fields provide excellent picnicking spots, but the river banks are high and steep, and the waters are deep, so the one or two places suitable for paddling and minnowing need searching out carefully!

Refreshments There are three public houses on the walk, all with beer gardens - the Swan at Swineford, the Upton Inn at Upton Cheyney, and the White Hart at Bitton. There is a picnic site at the start (and finish!) of the walk in Swineford, and another such site where the old railway crosses the Avon. All along the river bank are many spots which are ideal for picnicking.

FARMHOUSE, STANTON PRIOR

36

Route 8

4 miles

Stanton Prior, Marksbury, and Stantonbury Hill

Outline   Stanton Prior ~ Marksbury ~ Tucking Mill ~ Stantonbury Hill ~ Stanton Prior.

Summary   A slice of rich agricultural country just to the south-west of Bath. The walk follows generally flat field paths and tracks through an area of undulating countryside. There is, however, a strenuous climb towards the end with the ascent of Stantonbury Hill, a climb from the road level of 250 feet to the hilltop at 550 feet in under ½-mile. Following ploughing or heavy rain, the going underfoot will be very muddy, so appropriate footwear please!

Attractions   From Stanton Prior through to Tucking Mill, the walk passes through a rich, hard-working agricultural environment. At the outset, are the attractive buildings of Church Farm, housing milking parlours and cattle stalls. The path through to Marksbury crosses several fields, with a variety of uses - in September, when I last walked this route, there were cattle and sheep grazing, maize almost fully grown, winter wheat peeping up through the soil and the stubble remains of the summer's wheat harvest. From Marksbury through to Tucking Mill, ploughing was taking place and the deep red soil of the locality was being exposed. An excellent companion on this first stage of the walk would be the 'I-Spy On The Farm' booklet, with the sections on a mixed farm, an arable farm, hedgerows and cattle scoring especially heavily! Incidentally, the path actually passes directly through a complex of farm buildings on the edge of Marksbury, where you almost feel that you are trespassing!

From the A39 back to Stanton Prior, the path ascends Stantonbury Hill. This is the site of an Iron Age fort which, when combined with the neighbouring Winsbury Hill, provided a stronghold when the Britons rallied against the invading Saxons during the 5th century. Skirting the Iron Age fort are the remains of the Wansdyke, a frontier of bank and ditch built back in those distant days as a continuous line of defence. The Wansdyke stretched from south of Bristol out on to the Marlborough Downs, where very substantial remains are to be found east of Devizes. Stantonbury Hill today is heavily wooded, and it is not until the summit is reached that the vast views it commands open up. There is Kelston Round Hill, beyond the eastern fringes of Bristol, further still the Welsh Hills. It is a lonely, isolated spot strangely so close to the cities of Bath and Bristol.

Route 8

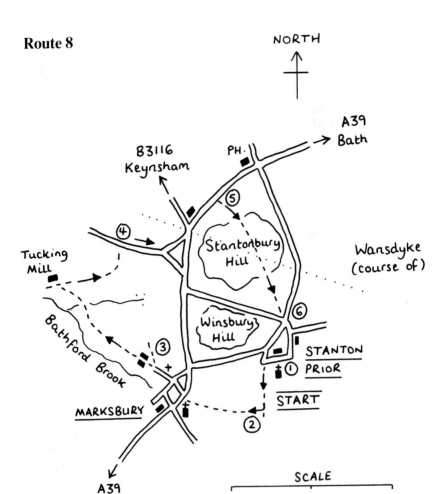

NORTH

A39
Bath

B3116
Keynsham

PH.

⑤

Stantonbury
Hill

Wansdyke
(course of)

④

Tucking
Mill

Winsbury
Hill

⑥

Bathford Brook

③

STANTON
PRIOR

START

MARKSBURY

②

A39
Wells

SCALE

0   ½   1mile

Route 8

Stanton Prior, Marksbury and Stantonbury Hill   4 miles

START   *Leave the A4 Bath to Bristol Road at Corston, and follow the A39 towards Marksbury. Just before the village of Marksbury, a turning to the left is sign-posted to 'Stanton Prior'. There is ample room for parking in Stanton Prior on the road outside the Church.*
(G.R. 678627)

ROUTE

1. *Walk along the main street in the village, with the Church on your left and Church Farm to your right. Where the road bends sharply to the right, you turn left over a gate into a field. Continue along the track across the field.*

2. *Look out for a stile on your right. Once across this stile, Marksbury Church is clearly visible about ½ mile distant. Walk directly towards the Church, crossing several obvious stiles on your way. A gate in the hedgerow brings you out on to the busy A39 at Marksbury, where the Church is a little way along on your left. The route through Marksbury is shown on the map, and a quiet cul-de-sac lane brings you to a large house and farm, fronted by a substantial millpond.*

3. *The obvious path is over a gate and along a track on your right. However, this is not our path! Our walk actually passes down through the farm-yard ahead, between barns and milking parlours. Once through the complex of farm buildings, the path is obvious, continuing for half-a-mile towards Tucking Mill, with Bathford Brook in the trees to the left. At Tucking Mill, follow the track to the right out on to a quiet country lane.*

4. *At the lane, turn right and continue along to the A39. Follow the A39 to the left, passing a garage on the left. In a short distance look for a gateway on the opposite side of the busy main road that marks the start of the climb up Stantonbury Hill.*

5. *A stile entering the woods half-way up the hill should be clearly visible. Head for this stile, and then follow the way-marked path (yellow arrows) up and across Stantonbury Hill. The descent of the far side of the hill brings Stanton Prior clearly into view, and obvious gateways in the hedgerows mark the right-of-way.*

6. *A gate brings the path out on to quiet country lanes, where the route back to the Church is as shown on the map.*

Public Transport   Public transport is seasonal, with a Bath to Weston-super-Mare bus service passing along the A39 through Marksbury only in the summer months.

Refreshments   There are no public houses directly on the route, the nearest being about 10 minutes walk along the A39 from the start of the path up Stantonbury Hill (see the map). The garage at the junction of the A39 with the B3116 does sell confectionery, crisps, drinks, etc.

BLAGDON VILLAGE AND LAKE

Route 9

Ubley, Blagdon and the Mendip Hills

Outline Ubley ~ Blagdon Lake ~ Blagdon ~ Mendip Hills ~ Ubley.

Summary Blagdon and Ubley are two attractive commuter-villages lying just 10 miles south of Bristol. Both lie just above the shores of Blagdon Lake, and are tucked in beneath the northern slopes of the Mendips. This walk first follows level field paths, close to the lake, before a steep ascent out of Blagdon takes you up on to the Mendip Hills. After level upland walking, with far-reaching views, the path descends steeply into Ubley. This is a strenuous walk that involves 700 feet of ascent from the lakeside.

Attractions Ubley is a quiet settlement, based around the Church of St. Bartholomew, the village green and a restored medieval cross. The 13th century church contains a chained copy of the Paraphrase of the Gospels by Erasmus, of 1552, a Jacobean wooden pulpit and parish chest. Nearby is Ubley trout hatchery, which breeds brown and rainbow trout and exports trout eggs all over the world. Unfortunately, the hatchery is not open to the public.

Blagdon Lake is a reservoir formed by damming the River Yeo in 1901. The dam now carries a road at the western end of the lake. This stretch of water is 1½ miles long and ½ mile wide, and covers 430 acres. It is rich in wildfowl - widgeon, teal and pochard in winter, great-crested grebe and ruddy duck in summer. Binoculars are essential since the path runs a little to the south of the lake, although keen ornithologists can obtain a closer view of the lake either from the dam or by obtaing a permit from the Bristol Waterworks Company (Woodford Lodge, Chew Stoke, Bristol).

The village of Blagdon stands on the lower slopes of the Mendips, its church being a prominent local landmark. A footpath from the church leads down to Timswell, where up to the 1920s the villagers had to collect their water. Blagdon today lies in the heart of Bristol's 'stockbroker belt', and empty cottages are quickly snapped up by Bristol business-men or retired people.

High above Blagdon, the walk crosses the northern slopes of the Mendip Hills. The views from Leaze Lane, an enclosed path high up on the hill-side, take in the Bristol Channel and the Welsh Coast to the west,

continued on page 44

Route 9

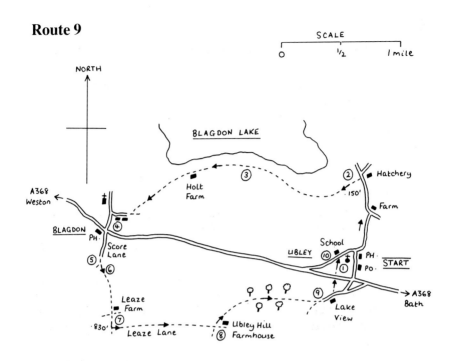

BLAGDON LAKE

42

Route 9

Ubley, Blagdon and the Mendip Hills   4½ miles

START   *Ubley lies between Blagdon and Compton Martin on the A368 Bath to Weston road. Coming from Blagdon, a minor road on the left leads down to the village church, outside of which the road is wide enough for parking.* (G.R. 529583)

ROUTE

1. *Turn left at the village cross, and walk down quiet country lanes as shown on the map until Ubley Hatchery is reached.*

2. *Almost opposite the Hatchery entrance is a signed public footpath. The path does not follow the Waterboard track to the lake, as notices clearly indicate. Rather, it passes through adjoining fields, directly parallel to the Waterboard's track.*

3. *The path through to Blagdon is so well way-marked that no description is necessary! It continues to run parallel to the Waterboard's track, which lies just over the hedgerow to the right, until Holt Farm is reached where the footpath veers up the hillside towards Blagdon.*

4. *The footpath reaches several large houses on the edge of Blagdon a little to the left of the church. Walk along past these houses into Blagdon itself, turning left when you reach Church Street. At the main road, the 'Live and Let Live' public house is directly opposite.*

5. *Alongside the pub, opposite Church Street, is Score Lane. Walk straight up this lane, until it becomes a path and reaches a stile. Cross the stile into open countryside.*

6. *Once over the stile, follow the left-hand hedgerow to the top of the hill, cross over the gate, and continue on up the lane towards Leaze Farm. At the 'crossroads' in front of the farm, continue straight across.*

7. *A little way up this path, turn left into an enclosed path - Leaze Lane. Follow this hill-top path for ¾ mile, with the last few hundred yards being across a field.*

8. *Slightly before Ubley Hill Farmhouse, a track - Ubley Drove - is reached. Turn left down this track, and follow it for close on one-mile through Ubley Wood. The path is steep and rocky, and can be muddy!*

9. *Once through the wood, you emerge on to a lane. In front of the cottage named 'Lake View', take the sign-posted footpath across the field to the main road below. Cross the main road, and almost opposite*

*is another sign-posted path. Follow this across a field, over a stile,
down past some bungalows, and out on to the road by Ubley School.*

10. *Turn right, and the church and your car are a few yards along the road
on the right-hand side.*

---

whilst below in the Yeo Valley lie Blagdon and Chew Valley Reservoirs,
Bristol's own Lake District! It is hard to believe that just beyond the hills
on the far side of the reservoirs lies a vast city, when all that can be seen
from the hills are scenes of rural peace and tranquility!

Leaze Lane is awash with wild flowers in summer - foxgloves,
knapweed, rosebay and trefoil, for example. The hedgerows that enclose
the path here do unfortunately block the fine view, so it is important to
take the opportunity to peer over every gate or gap that occurs. Ubley
Wood is a deciduous woodland, much akin to the woodland at Ebor
Gorge (see Route 10), not surprisingly, bearing in mind that both lie on
the same limestone outcrop that constitutes the Mendips.

Refreshments Half-way around the walk, at Blagdon, is the 'Live and
Let Live' public-house. The sign outside boasts of food and a beer
garden, with children very welcome. This is probably preferable to a
picnic on this particular walk, because heavy ruck-sacks are probably best
left at home!

HART'S TONGUE FERN

Ebbor Gorge, Mendips

Outline   A circular walk around Ebbor Gorge, on the Mendip Hills
above Wells.

Summary   A short but strenuous walk around Ebor Gorge, a fine
example of a Mendip Valley. The walk does involve a scramble up
through the gorge itself, that the youngsters will thoroughly enjoy but
which is best left alone by Grandma! There is a much shorter and
consequently less spectacular route, which avoids the scramble, and this
shorter alternative is shown on the map. The viewpoint above the gorge is
dangerous, being directly above vertical cliffs - please keep away from the
edge! The remainder of the walk is along well-marked woodland paths.

Attractions   Ebbor Gorge is a National Nature Reserve, managed by the
Nature Conservancy Council and leased from the National Trust. The
gorge is typical of limestone country - it was carved out by an ancient river
that has long since disappeared beneath the permeable limestone. Within
the gorge, joints and fissures have been enlarged by the passage of
rain-water, leaving behind small caves and rock shelters where the
remains of reindeer, bears, wolves and lemmings have been found by
archaeologists. Neolithic man also sought shelter in these caves around
3000 BC, and his various remains - bones, tools and ornaments - can be
seen in Wells Museum.

   The gorge is surrounded by deciduous woodland, which is both
carefully managed and conserved by the Nature Conservancy Council.
The woodland at the foot of the gorge contains ash, elm, beech and oak,
together with herbaceous plants such as dog's mercury, enchanter's
nightshade and hart's tongue fern. Badgers are plentiful here, and you
may notice their tracks left when in search of berries and beetles. On the
rather more rocky slopes of the gorge itself, vegetation characteristic of
such an upland environment is found - dogwood, spindle, whitebeam and
buckthorn. The excellent display centre next to the car-park gives a full
account of the natural history and geology of the area.

   The view from the top of the cliffs above the gorge is truly
spectacular. Here the path is some 800 feet above sea-level, and spread
out panoramically beneath are the Somerset Levels, Wookey and Wells
to the east, and the Tor at Glastonbury standing out as a prominent
land-mark. In the background, far away to the south and the west, lie the
Quantock Hills and Exmoor.

continued on page 48

45

Route 10

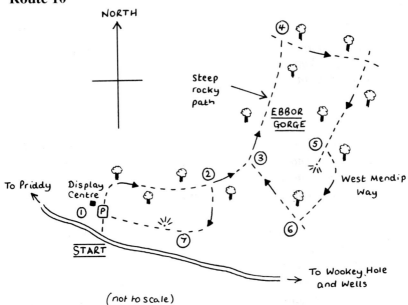

NORTH

Steep
rocky
path

EBBOR
GORGE

To Priddy

Display
Centre

① P

START

West Mendip
Way

② ③ ④ ⑤ ⑥ ⑦

To Wookey Hole
and Wells

(not to scale)

NATIONAL TRUST MONUMENT

Route 10

Ebbor Gorge, Mendips

2 miles

START   *Ebbor Gorge lies just off of the Wookey Hole to Priddy minor road. Wookey Hole, being a popular tourist attraction, is well sign-posted from Wells. At Ebbor, there is ample parking.* (G.R. 520485)

ROUTE

Both the routes around the gorge are way-marked, the main route with red arrows, the shorter route with black arrows. Detailed directions are therefore superfluous!

1. *A stone stile out of the car-park, followed by a stepped path down to the foot of the gorge.*

2. *Follow the signs for the car-park to complete the shorter circular route that avoids the gorge.*

3. *A distinct left turn up into the gorge.*

4. *At the top of gorge, a right-turn at the junction of paths.*

5. *Walk to the view-point over-looking the gorge, before retracing your steps and continuing the main walk.*

6. *At the bottom of the stepped path, turn right. A sign post indicates that you have just walked a section of the West Mendip Way, a long-distance path that runs from Wells to Weston.*

7. *A stone that commemorates the presentation of the gorge to the National Trust on the 17th of May 1967 by a Mrs. G. W. Hodgkinson. The stone fittingly looks back towards the actual gorge.*

NB.   *On the return leg of the journey, if you cannot find the red arrows, then simply follow the signs for the car-park.*

On returning to the car-park, there are many well-laid-out picnic areas, where the family can just relax or play or enjoy the views. Not five minutes drive away is Wookey Hole, with its cavern, its waxworks, its collection of fair-ground memorabilia and its paper making factory, all open to the public. Wookey in turn is almost a suburb of the tiny City of Wells, with its Cathedral, Bishop's Palace and moat, where the resident swans actually ring a bell each afternoon to announce to the world that it is feeding time! Within this small compact area of the Mendips, there are ample attractions for a family day-out.

The Mendip Hills,   average height between 900 and 1000 feet, run for some 30 miles across the northern boundary of Somerset. The whole is a limestone mass, with the most notable features being the cave systems and underground caverns carved out of the limestone by the action of water. The bleak and lonely landscape rises to a maximum height of 1067 feet at Blackdown, on the hills above Burrington Combe. It was in a rock cleft at Burrington that the Reverend Augustus Toplady composed the hymn 'Rock of Ages' whilst sheltering from a thunderstorm.

Refreshments   There are no refreshment facilities at Ebbor, other than well-laid out picnic areas. For those demanding something more substantial, then a short ride to Wookey or Wells will provide an abundance of pubs, restaurants, cafes, tea-rooms....and crowds!

CHEDDAR GORGE

Route 11

Cheddar and the Gorge

Outline   Black Rock ~ Cheddar ~ Black Rock.

Summary   The heavy volume of traffic that passes through Cheddar Gorge, especially during the summer months, makes walking along the road beneath the cliffs an utterly miserable experience! Places like Cheddar convince me that the British public are wholesale sufferers from agoraphobia, this wonder having to be viewed without venturing out from the car! The walk follows paths atop the cliffs on both sides of the Gorge, high above the road with its noise and fumes. From Black Rock, there is a short steep climb to gain height, before a steady descent down the eastern side of the Gorge into Cheddar. The path is unfenced, and the drop over the cliff-edge several hundred feet - enough said! The return to Black Rock along the western side of the Gorge starts with a mile of hard uphill walking, before level paths and glorious views are obtained.

Attractions   Cheddar Gorge is one of the most famous natural features in the British Isles. The Gorge was carved out of the limestone by rivers that now pass deep underground, leaving vertical cliffs of up to 450 feet in height. The path from Black Rock to Cheddar passes literally along the top of these cliffs, and brings what must be one of the most dramatic views in the South of England. In the foreground is Cheddar and the Gorge, whilst beyond lie the Somerset Levels, Glastonbury Tor, Brent Knoll, Bridgwater Bay and the Quantock Hills.

Although off the actual walk, there are several attractions in Cheddar itself. These include Gough's Cave, Cox's Cave and Waterfall Cave, all open to the public and containing fantastic stalactite and stalagmite formations.

The climb back up to Black Rock from Cheddar along the western side of the Gorge passes through the National Trust's Cheddar Cliffs. Once sufficient height (and aching leg muscles) are secured, the precariousness of the route taken earlier down into Cheddar becomes obvious as remote figures walking the path on the opposite side of the Gorge come into view.

Refreshments   Half-way around the walk is Cheddar itself, where there are chip-shops, pubs, cafes, tea-shops, etc. Cheddar itself is commercialised beyond description! If you wish to pass through the

continued on page 52

Route 11

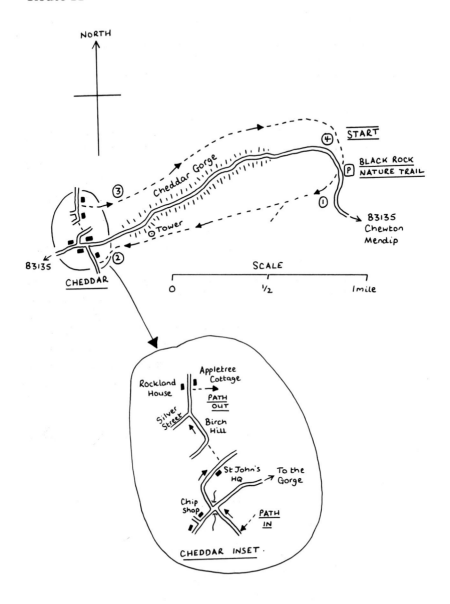

NORTH

START

BLACK ROCK
NATURE TRAIL

③

Cheddar Gorge

④

P

①

B3135
Chewton
Mendip

○ Tower

B3135

②

CHEDDAR

SCALE

0   ½   1 mile

Appletree
Cottage

Rockland
House

PATH
OUT

Silver
Street

Birch
Hill

St John's
HQ

To the
Gorge

Chip
Shop

PATH
IN

CHEDDAR INSET.

Route 11

Cheddar and the Gorge

4 miles

START *At the top of Cheddar Gorge is the Black Rock Nature Trail. Just outside the entrance to the trail is parking space on the B3135 road for approximately a dozen vehicles.* (G.R. 482545)

ROUTE

1. *Opposite the parking space, across the busy B3135 road, is a West Mendip Way marker post sign-posted 'Draycott'. Follow this path, initially up a steep woodland path, and then on to the high-ground above the Gorge. A short way on, the West Mendip Way forks off to the left, and you follow the path along the edge of the gorge. Be warned, the drop down to the road is sheer and unfenced! Pass to the left of the observation-tower alongside Jacob's Ladder, and continue down the woodland path towards Cheddar village.*

2. *Rather than a tedious list of directions and street names, the route through Cheddar has been drawn as a detailed inset map.*

3. *The return path up the opposite side of the Gorge lies on land known as 'Cheddar Cliffs', which is National Trust Property. The path is obvious, and has been well way-marked by the Trust. The first half-a-mile is up an extremely steep path, with hedgerows either side, meaning that there are no views to compensate you for your efforts....the views come later!*

4. *At the top of the Gorge, the path drops down steeply to the B3135 road, where you turn left back to the Black Rock parking space.*

GREAT CRESTED GREBE
(Route 9)

built-up area as quickly as possible, there is fortunately a chip-shop and a grocers lying almost on the route itself - see the inset map. The high ground way up on top of the gorge itself provides superb picnicking spots providing that the wind isn't too fierce!

BURRINGTON COMBE

Burrington Combe and High Mendip

Outline   Burrington Combe ~ West Twin Brook ~ Blackdown ~ Burrington Combe.

Summary   A spectacular walk from the limestone cliffs of Burrington Combe to the highest point on Mendip, Beacon Batch, 1067 feet above sea-level. The first mile is hard-going, an ascent of some six-or-seven hundred feet on to the top of Blackdown. The path is then level to Beacon Batch itself, with the return to Burrington downhill. The weather on Blackdown can be atrocious, and the going underfoot wet and muddy, which makes this one walk where boots and waterproofs are a must!

Attractions   The most obvious absentee from areas of carboniferous limestone is surface-water. Just where are the rivers and streams? The answer is simple - underground! The mild solution of carbonic-acid found in rainwater dissolves the cracks and joints found in the limestone. This forms an elaborate network of caves, pot-holes, and underground passages, into which have disappeared most of the rivers and streams. Several features common to such an environment can be seen along the early stages of this walk.

Opposite the car-park is the famous 'Rock of Ages'. An inscription on the rock reads:

ROCK OF AGES
This rock derives its name
from the well-known hymn written about 1762
by the Rev. A. M. Toplady
Who was inspired whilst sheltering in this cleft during a storm.

The cleft? A joint in the limestone widened by the action of the slightly acidic rain!

A little way up the Combe, on the left-hand side, is Aveline's Hole. This small cave is again the result of acidic rainwater reacting with the limestone. Whilst rabbit-hunting in 1797, two men discovered this cave together with its contents - 50 human skeletons! It was an ancient Stone-Age burial chamber.

Shortly, the path turns off the road and the course of West Twin Brook is followed. Following rainfall, the stream can be seen flowing into a small pot-hole just up from the road. The stream was actually diverted

continued on page 56

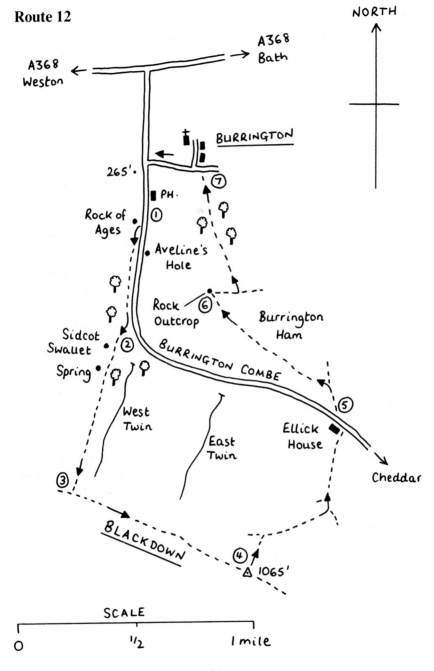

Route 12

NORTH

A368
Bath

A368
Weston

† BURRINGTON

265'.

⑦

PH.

①

Rock of
Ages

Aveline's
Hole

Rock
Outcrop ⑥

Burrington
Ham

Sidcot
Swallet ②

BURRINGTON COMBE

Spring

West
Twin

East
Twin

Ellick
House ⑤

③

Cheddar

BLACKDOWN

④

△ 1065'

SCALE

0   ½   1 mile

Route 12
Burrington Combe and High Mendip   4 miles

START   *Burrington Combe lies just ½ mile off the A368 Weston-super-Mare to Bath Road. A little way past the Burrington Freehouse, directly opposite the Rock of Ages, is a parking area and toilets.* (G.R. 476588)

ROUTE

1. *Cross the road to pick up the path that passes in front of the Rock of Ages. Follow this path up through the Combe, passing Aveline's Hole, with the road always at hand to your left. Shortly after Aveline's Hole, a well-worn track on your right leads up the West Twin Valley, and you begin the steady ascent of Blackdown!*

2. *The path, which is now rocky underfoot, actually forms the bed of West Twin Brook. Following rainfall, you will actually be walking in a fast-flowing but shallow stream! Continue up the stream-bed, until West Twin passes into some bushes to your left, and the path veers off to the right past a spring. Beyond the spring, the path steepens considerably and you pass on to the open ground that forms Blackdown. The break from limestone to sandstone is noticeable as the vegetation abruptly changes to sparse bracken and heather. Continue up the hillside-path, refusing any left or right turns, and all the while keeping West Twin slightly to your left in the dip.*

3. *After almost one mile of hard walking, you reach a 'junction' high up on the top of Blackdown. Turn left, and follow the upland path to the triangulation pillar of Beacon Batch, just over 1000 feet above sea-level. The pillar is not visible immediately, so keep your eyes open!*

4. *At the pillar, turn left and head off down the hillside, looking for the distant Ellick House. When you reach Ellick House, and the road from Burrington to Cheddar, turn left. A short distance down the road will bring you to a parking area.*

5. *Cross the road, pass through the parking area, and take the path that heads back in the direction of Burrington. The road will be below you and to your left, with Blackdown rising impressively in the background. Continue along this path, forking left at an early junction, and continue on for half-a-mile until you reach a rock outcrop.*

6. *At this outcrop, take the right-hand path that almost heads back in the direction that you have just come from …. almost, but not quite! Take the first turn on your left, and pass through woodland until you reach a quiet country lane.*

7. *Turn left, continue down the lane, avoiding the right-turn into Burrington village itself. The lane shortly brings you out on to the main road through the Combe, where you turn left back to the car-park.*

Public Transport A seasonal Bath to Weston-super-Mare service passes 'Burrington Turn', half-a-mile from the start of the walk. Public transport, however, is on the whole poor and details should be checked with Bristol Omnibus.

---

into the pot-hole by the Water Authorities, since its original course took it out on to the road where it regularly caused flooding! A little further up the stream-bed, lying to the right up above the path, is Sidcot Swallet, a pot-hole popular with today's cavers.

The change in geology as the path passes on to the sandstone of Blackdown is marked by the change in vegetation. The more acid soil of this upland area supports mainly bracken and heather, with a plentiful supply of bilberry plants lurking at ground level! Many theories surround the rows of small mounds lying either side of the path atop Blackdown. The most plausible is that these grassed-over stones were designed to destroy enemy planes tempted to land on this flat upland during the 1939-45 war.

From Beacon Batch the views are immense and really defy description. The Bristol Channel, the Welsh Hills, Chew and Blagdon Reservoirs, Exmoor.....the landmarks are many. It is worth taking a map with you to try and identify towns, villages and other such landmarks. This is certainly a spot to pause and enjoy!

From Ellick House to Burrington, the path passes over 'The Ham'. This is an open stretch of limestone upland, coarse-grass, scattered bushes and shrubs, from where a fine view of Blackdown can be obtained.

Refreshments At the start of the walk is the Burrington Freehouse, where snacks, hot-meals and drinks are available. Beacon Batch would be an excellent spot to devour a packed-lunch on a fine day, as would 'The Ham'. Should youngsters be tired after descending Blackdown and reaching Ellick House, an adult could walk quickly down the Combe via the road to collect the car, whilst the rest of the group rest at the car-park at the top of the Combe.

Brean Down, near Weston-super-Mare

Outline   A circular perambulation of Brean Down.

Summary   A circular walk around Brean Down, a limestone outcrop in the Bristol Channel that is a western extension of the great limestone chain of the Mendips. There are two fairly steep ascents - at the start of the walk up on to the Down itself, and from the fort at the western end of the Down back up to the summit. There is also a steep descent at the end of the walk, down a flight of steps back to the car-park. The paths generally, however, are level and well-defined.

Attractions   Along the Avon and Somerset coast are a collection of busy seaside resorts - Burnham-on-Sea, Berrow, Brean and Weston-super-Mare. Rising formidably between Weston and Brean is the massive limestone outcrop of Brean Down, 320 feet high, 1½ miles in length and just ⅓ mile wide. It is a haven of peace and tranquility along an otherwise commercially over-developed coastline.

The views from the Down are truly impressive - Weston to the north, the Brecon Beacons to the west along with the Welsh coastal towns of Swansea, Newport and Cardiff, to the south lies Hinkley Point Nuclear Power Station and the towns of Watchet and Minehead, rising behind them are the Quantock Hills and Exmoor, and to the east lie the Somerset Levels, with Mendip, Glastonbury Tor and Brent Knoll rising as noticeable landmarks. These places are shown as a topograph attached to the main map.

The whole of the Down is protected by the National Trust, and has been scheduled as a Site of Special Scientific Interest by the Nature Conservancy Council for its exceptional natural history. The Down is also an ancient monument as scheduled by the Department of the Environment for its archaeological remains.

The flora covers both common and rare species, with the white rock rose, the dwarf sedge, the goldilocks and the Somerset hair-grass coming into the latter category. The bird-life of the Down includes sky-larks, meadow-pipits, linnets and stonechats, with waders such as the dunlin and the oyster-catcher being found at the water's edge.

The archaeological remains cover a hill-fort dating from 150 BC, the remains of a Roman Temple and its associated Field Systems, and the

continued on page 60

Route 13

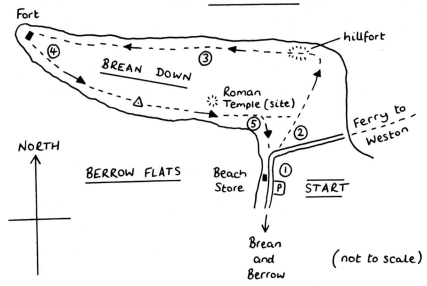

WESTON BAY

Fort

④

BREAN DOWN

③

hillfort

Roman Temple (site)

Ferry to Weston

NORTH

BERROW FLATS

⑤

②

Beach Store

①
P

START

Brean and Berrow

(not to scale)

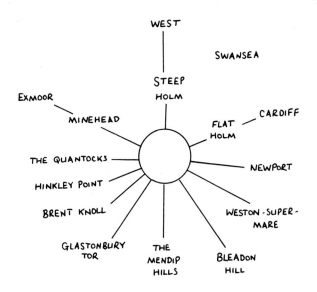

WEST

SWANSEA

STEEP HOLM

EXMOOR

MINEHEAD

FLAT HOLM

CARDIFF

THE QUANTOCKS

NEWPORT

HINKLEY POINT

BRENT KNOLL

WESTON-SUPER-MARE

GLASTONBURY TOR

THE MENDIP HILLS

BLEADON HILL

BREAN DOWN : AUTHOR'S TOPOGRAPH.

Route 13

Brean Down near Weston-super-Mare   3 miles

START   *Heading south out of Weston along the A370, the Brean road is a right-turn at Lympsham. From here, it really is a question of following the signs as you travel along the narrow and windy roads that cross the marsh to Brean Down. The alternative is to head for Burnham-on-Sea and to follow the Berrow and Brean signs. The road through to Brean Down is a cul-de-sac ending in a car-park by the beach shop at Brean Down. (G.R. 297586)*

ROUTE

1. *From the car-park, follow the lane sign-posted 'To the Ferry'. A little way along this lane, a path bears up on to the Down on the left.*

2. *Follow this path up on to Brean Down. (Do not gain access to the Down via the steps - that is the return journey's end!) At the top of this path is an information board, and wide-ranging views across Weston Bay.*

3. *Head to the western end of Brean Down along the lower path that keeps to the Weston side of the hill. Do not attempt to take any right turns (into the sea!) or left turns up on to the summit of the Down.*

4. *From the fort, follow the path up the ridge to the summit of Brean Down at Crook Peak, marked by a triangulation pillar. From here, continue walking back along the ridge towards the beach.*

5. *Immediately above the car-park, a right-turn brings you to a steep flight of steps, which you follow back down to the start of the walk and the beach shop.*

FLY AGARIC (Route 14)

59

substantial Brean Down Fort at the western end of the outcrop, built in 1870 as protection against possible invasion by Napoleon III. The site contained seven 7-inch rifle muzzle-loading canon. It was more recently manned by 571 Regiment Coast Artillery, Western Command, following the outbreak of World War II. The strategic position, protecting the Severn Estuary, and the port installations at Cardiff, Newport, Bristol and Avonmouth, make it an obvious locational choice.

Back in Brean itself, youngsters will enjoy the sands, although being an estuary means an abundance of mud! There are some small rocks and rock pools below the southern cliffs of Brean Down for crabbing, but again mind the mud! Just beyond the beach-shop and cafe is a small Tropical Bird Garden, although if Tropical Birds are your forte, the bird gardens at Rode (Route 2) are much more substantial.

Refreshments The beach shop at Brean has a cafe above it. The beach and the Down itself provide excellent picnicking locations.

NIGHTINGALE VALLEY

Route 14   4 miles

Leigh Woods and the Avon Gorge

Outline   Leigh Woods ~ Paradise Bottom ~ Avon Gorge ~ Nightingale Valley ~ Leigh Woods.

Summary   Pleasant walking through woodland bordering the Avon Gorge, and along the river bank through the gorge itself. Initially, there is a gentle descent through Leigh Woods, then a flat path beside the river, and finally a relatively steep climb up through Nightingale Valley, ascending some 250 feet. Unfortunately, the riverside path through the gorge is far from peaceful, with heavy traffic using the A4 on the opposite bank of the river, but this is more than compensated for by the spectacular view of the Clifton Suspension Bridge almost 250 feet above the river level!

Attractions   Leigh Woods is a fine area of generally deciduous woodland managed by the Forestry Commission. This is a fine spot for progressing towards the Award of Merit should you be the owner of an I-Spy Trees book ..... or for the less serious it is a great place for a quiet game of hide-and-seek!

In the Avon Gorge, the River Avon is almost at the end of its 75-mile journey from either Sherston or Tetbury, depending upon which tributary you regard as the source! The Avon here is both tidal and navigable. Commercial traffic, however, is virtually zero, since the port facilities in the heart of Bristol were officially closed in 1971. Shipping activity is now concentrated at Avonmouth, eight miles downstream from the centre of Bristol, where the Avon joins the sea. Here, the much larger oceangoing vessels can be accomodated, leaving only the occasional sand-dredger to venture up the river to Bristol.

The Gorge is made up of carboniferous limestone, overlaid by a layer of millstone grit. On the far bank of the river, beneath the Suspension Bridge, the strata or layers of this limestone can clearly be seen to be dipping at an angle of 30 degrees. The tunnel on the A4 at this point is to protect traffic from rock-falls.

The Suspension Bridge, like many other items of industrial history in Bristol, was designed by Brunel. It was opened in 1861, cost £100,000 to construct, stands 245 feet above the river, and has a span of 702 feet. It is notorious for suicides and attempted suicides, with the most

continued on page 64

Route 14

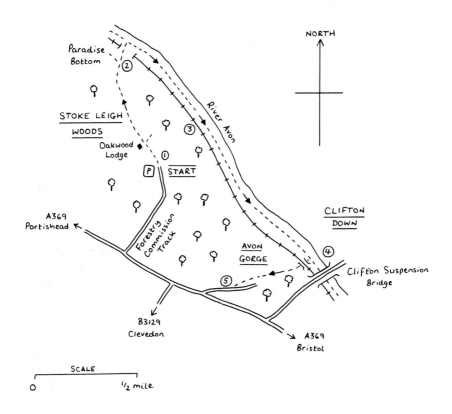

Route 14

Leigh Woods and the Avon Gorge 4 miles

START   *Take the A369 Bristol to Portishead Road, either from Ashton Gate or by crossing the Clifton Suspension Bridge. Shortly after the traffic lights where the B3129 turns off to Clevedon and Weston, a sign on the right indicates the entrance to Stoke Leigh Woods. Drive down the Forestry Commission Track to the car-park, some 800 yards from the main road. (At the car-park is a display board that describes two walks through the Woods, should you want something rather shorter than the walk described here!) (G.R. 553737)*

ROUTE

1. *Follow the Forestry Commission Track downhill for just over ½ mile, ignoring any intermediate turnings off the main path. You are in fact following the 'red route' described on the Commission's information board.*

2. *Where the track forks, take the right branch turning off the red route. This path takes you over a stone wall that forms the boundary of the forest, over a tunnel containing the Bristol to Portishead railway, and out on to the Avon Walkway where you turn right.*

3. *Follow the Avon Walkway through the Gorge for close on two miles. This level path is also used by cyclists, so take care!*

4. *Just before the Suspension Bridge, turn right under the railway and follow a path up through 'Nightingale Valley'.*

5. *This path emerges at the official entrance to the Avon Gorge Nature Reserve. I would recommend that you all wait here whilst the driver walks up the road to the A369, and returns to the car-park as shown on the map to collect the car. This last short section of the walk contains a stretch of busy road which isn't much fun to walk, and it should only be a 15-20 minute wait before the driver returns with the car.*

Public Transport   The regular Bristol to Portishead service passes the entrance to Stoke Leigh Woods and the start of the walk.

extraordinary being a Victorian lady whose attempt was foiled when her billowing skirts acted as a parachute, and she descended slowly and safely to land in the soft mud below - the tide was out!

The final leg of the walk from the river up through Nightingale Valley lies within the Avon Gorge National Nature Reserve. This is one of the most important woodland sites on lowland carboniferous limestone in the country, and contains two unique species - the Bristol Whitebeam and the Bristol Rock Cress. The Reserve leaflet, available at the entrance to the Reserve (point 5 on the map), contains illustrations of these species and lots more information besides. Easier to find, and perhaps of more general interest, are the rich collection of fungi in the Reserve. During the Autumn months, many colourful specimens appear, such as the poisonous red and white fly agaric.

At the end of the walk, it is worth driving over the Suspension Bridge, and parking on the far side to visit one or two attractions. For a very modest fee, pedestrians can cross the bridge itself - well worth doing if you have a head for heights and want to obtain a bird's eye view of the walk. Nearby, is the 'observatory', constructed from an old windmill and containing a camera obscura that projects a 360 degree view of the City of Bristol. Down below the observatory is a pot-hole that brings the intrepid explorer into a caged-cave clinging on to the cliff-side high above the river. The admission charged to these two attractions is less modest than that for crossing the bridge, and on balance - for sheer excitement - I would favour the cave!

Refreshments   There are no refreshment facilities on this walk. The best spot for a picnic would be in Nightingale Valley, the riverbank itself not offering any suitable sites. A little way along the A369 towards Portishead lies the village of Abbots Leigh, with a public-house 'The George' actually on the main road. The best plan, however, is to enjoy a picnic on Clifton Down after the walk, having first driven across the Suspension Bridge.

Moorend, Bury Hill and the Bristol Frome

Outline   Whiteshill Common ~ The Dingle ~ Bury Hill ~ Moorend ~ Whiteshill Common.

Summary   A short, gentle stroll centred on the River Frome, a tributary of the Bristol Avon, as it passes through countryside so close to the heart of Bristol. There are no real climbs on the walk, which follows a mixture of field-paths, riverside tracks and quiet lanes. An ideal walk if you have younger children who enjoy walking, but as yet lack the stamina for longer perambulation!

Attractions   Whiteshill Common is a flat grassed area of common land on which, in theory, local farmers can freely graze their livestock. In practice, the proximity of traffic and the regular use of the Common by football and cricket teams, would make 'common grazing' a hazardous occupation! It is an ideal spot for families to picnic, or to play games - so come prepared with footballs, cricket-bats and the like.

The River Frome, not to be confused with the Frome down in Somerset, has its source in Dodington Park, and passes through Iron Acton, Frampton Cotterell, Winterbourne and Frenchay, before joining the Avon right in the centre of Bristol. The word Frome means 'brisk' and this short river certainly lives up to its name as it tumbles over the local Pennant Sandstone that bedecks its bed. The Local Authority have created 'The River Frome Walkway', a linked series of footpaths that follow the river from Bristol out beyond Frampton towards its source. The whole path is well-signed, and part of its course is followed on this walk. A map and guide to this Walkway are obtainable from Northavon District Council at the Council Offices, Chipping Sodbury near Bristol. A small charge is made for the leaflet.

The first section of the Frome that is followed passes through old quarries where pennant sandstone was once extensively worked. Along the walk, the importance of this stone as a building material can be seen in many of the old cottages and walls. It has a rather sombre look, its colour varying from grey to dark red. The old quarries have now either been in-filled with local refuse and returned to agricultural use, or lie overgrown, often with blackberry bushes. This is superb blackberrying country, so if you pick the right season, come armed with punnets, baskets and plastic tubs!

continued on page 68

Route 15

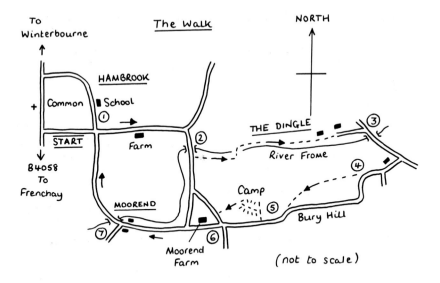

The Walk

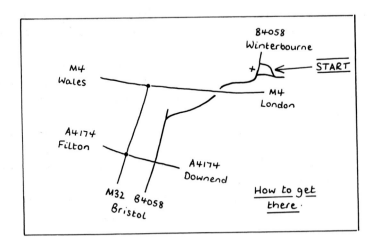

How to get there.

Route 15

Moorend, Bury Hill and the Bristol Frome   2 miles

START   *Whiteshill Common is just 5 miles from the centre of Bristol. The inset map shows its location relative to the nearby M32 motorway. Ample parking exists on the Common, and for the start of the walk, it is assumed that you are parked outside of the village school.* (G.R. 646793)

ROUTE

1. *With the school on your left, walk along the road to a crossroads and turn left into Worral's Lane. Walk down this road, past the entrance to Waterfalls Farm on your right, to the bottom of a gentle hill where a road forks off to the right.*

2. *Turn right, cross the River Frome, and almost immediately take the path on the left-hand side signposted 'Frome Valley Walkway'. Follow this path, keeping the river on your left, to a footbridge. Cross the river, and continue along the riverside path until you emerge on to a road - The Dingle. Follow this for a few hundred yards to a road junction.*

3. *Turn right, crossing the Frome, and take the first road on the right - Bury Hill. Continue up the hill, avoiding any left-turns, until at the top of the incline a stone stile appears immediately in front of you.*

4. *Cross this stile, and continue across fields with the hedgerow on your right until another stile brings you out on to a road. Turn right along this road.*

5. *Look for a footpath on the right, that heads up towards Bury Hill Camp. Take this track, and soon on the left a stile takes the path into the Camp itself. The path goes diagonally across the Camp to a house on the far side. Cross the stile in front of the house, and turn left down a lane.*

6. *Follow this lane, past old quarry workings, until it joins a road. Turn left, and shortly - at a crossroads - turn right down past Moorend Farm. Follow this road down to the Frome, and continue along the road keeping the river on your right.*

7. *Shortly, a road forks off on the left, but you carry on, round a bend, and up a hill - known locally as 'Jack and Jill Hill' -which takes you back up to Whiteshill Common.*

Public Transport   The regular Bristol Omnibus services from Bristol to Winterbourne and Frampton Cotterell all pass Whiteshill Common.

Bury Hill Camp is quite substantial, covering some 5½ acres. On three sides, the two ramparts are clearly visible; quarrying has removed the ramparts on the fourth side. Excavations have shown evidence of Roman occupation, although the site was certainly occupied even earlier. The Iberians seem to have used the site in the 8th century BC, followed by Celtic tribes.

Moorend Farm, dated 1676, is a fine old building. Particularly impressive are its gabled roof and its stone construction. Richard Champion, England's first porcelain manufacturer, lived there for some time.

Just past Moorend Farm, the Frome is rejoined, and at this point the lane forms part of the Frome Valley Walkway. Just before the road climbs up the hill back to the Common, there is an easily accessible section of the river, which is both shallow and safe. This part of the river is excellent for paddling and minnowing, and in the middle of the waterway lie a couple of small islands - great fun for exploring. Don't forget your towels!

Refreshments   There are no refreshment facilities on this walk, although the Common and Bury Hill Camp would both make good picnicking spots. Just off the walk, at the bottom of Whiteshill as you follow the B4058 back towards Bristol, are a steak-house and a pub.

SALMON PUTCHERS ON THE SEVERN

Route 16

Oldbury and the Severn

Outline   Oldbury ~ Littleton Pill ~ Oldbury Pill ~ Oldbury.

Summary   A gentle stroll along flat paths that border the River Severn. The only climb, a very modest ascent, is to reach St. Arilda's Church at Oldbury, from where fine views of the locality can be obtained from the comfort of a churchyard seat!

Attractions   Although some distance from the river, Oldbury would literally have been 'on-Severn' in centuries past, when floods frequently swamped the local low-lying land. To the south of the village lies St. Arilda's Church, elevated on a small hill or knoll, from where a fine view is obtained. Downstream lies the Severn Bridge, and upstream the concrete towers of Oldbury Nuclear Power Station. Across the river lie Chepstow, the Forest of Dean and the foothills of the Welsh Mountains.

Whale Wharf on Littleton Pill is so named because in 1885, a whale became stranded there on the outgoing tide. This was once a tiny port, importing Welsh coal and exporting local bricks. Today it is little more than a muddy inlet. Close at hand lies the Severn Bridge, carrying the M4 London-to-South Wales motorway across the river. Built between 1961 and 1966 at a cost of £8 million, it has a main span of 3240 feet, a total length of almost one-mile, towers 400 feet high and its support cables are 20 inches thick.

The River Severn rises on the eastern slopes of Plynlimmon, deep in Central Wales, from where its 210 mile journey to the Bristol Channel commences. At Oldbury, the river is tidal, and at low tide the racks of conical-shaped baskets or 'putchers' used by local salmon fishermen should be visible. The open ends of these putchers usually face upstream to capture the salmon on the ebb tide as they migrate through the estuary. This technique of fishing has prehistoric origins and is unique to the Severn. The estuary supports large numbers of birds which are adapted to feed on the abundant supply of small, mud-dwelling creatures. Waders, such as the dunlin, are especially common during the winter months. Lists of species to spot would be futile, with so much depending upon the tides and the seasons, so come armed with your binoculars and bird-spotting books!

continued on page 72

Route 16

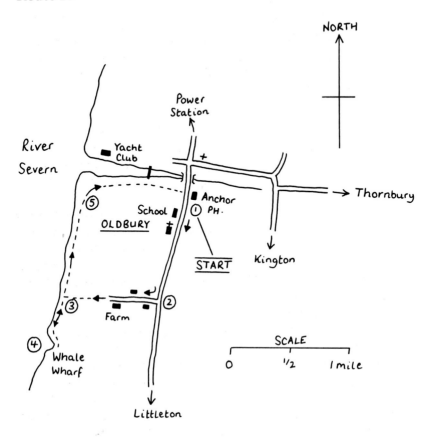

NORTH

River Severn

Power Station

Yacht Club

+

→ Thornbury

⑤

Anchor PH.

School

①

OLDBURY

+

START

↓ Kington

③

②

Farm

SCALE

0   ½   1 mile

④

Whale Wharf

↓ Littleton

Route 16

Oldbury and the Severn   3½ miles

START   *Take the B4061 road through Thornbury, and on the northern outskirts of the town, a minor road on the left is sign-posted to Oldbury. In the village, turn left at the cross-roads and park on the verges somewhere near the Anchor Public House. (G.R. 608923)*

ROUTE

1. *Head south, away from the village, along the road that climbs a gentle hill to the school and St. Arilda's Church. You will undoubtedly want to take the short detour into the churchyard to admire the fine views of the Severn from this 'church-on-a-hill'. Continue on down the road in the general direction of the Severn Bridge.*

2. *Shortly, a lane forks off to the right just past a bus-stop. Follow this lane, sign-posted as a no through road, until it becomes a track just beyond a farm. Follow this track on to the banks of the Severn.*

3. *If you want a shorter walk, turn right at the river and follow the path back to Oldbury. For the main walk, turn left and continue to Whale Wharf on Littleton Pill. This stretch of path gives fine views downstream to the Severn Bridge.*

4. *From Littleton Wharf, retrace your steps and head back upstream towards Oldbury. The path actually runs along the top of the sea-defences. Look out for the salmon putchers if it is low-tide.*

5. *The route back to Oldbury is obvious, following the sea-defences to the Yacht Club, and then the path that runs parallel to Oldbury Pill and along its banks back into the village. The last few hundred yards are through fields where stiles clearly indicate the right-of-way.*

Public Transport Bristol Omnibus operate buses from Bristol to Thornbury, from where an irregular minibus service runs down to Oldbury. In many ways, this walk is based on too remote a spot to make public transport a viable alternative to the car for a family!

Oldbury Nuclear Power Station was constructed between 1961 and 1965. The location is ideal insofar as a band of Keuper Marl runs 13 feet below the ground at this point to provide firm foundations. Further, a rock-shelf below the river helped with the construction of a 380-acre reservoir actually in the Severn itself, where even at ebb tide five feet of water is still held for cooling purposes. The towers holding the actual reactors are 60 feet high.

Refreshments   The Anchor Public House in Oldbury-on-Severn has a large beer garden, and would provide an excellent place for refreshment after a pleasant morning's stroll along the river. Equally, anywhere along the banks of the Severn would make an excellent picnicking spot, with fine views across the water.

FOOTBRIDGE OVER THE FROME (Route 2)

MOOREND FARM (Route 15)

Appendices

Approximate mileage of each Walk from Bristol and Bath via main roads.

Route	Bristol	Bath
1	30	18
2	25	12
3	25	15
4	18	5
5	18	5
6	20	4
7	6	6
8	10	7
9	20	18
10	25	27
11	25	25
12	18	22
13	25	35
14	3	15
15	5	20
16	15	25

ROUTES IN ORDER OF DIFFICULTY

To the experienced walker only one or two of the walks on Mendip would be at all strenuous. However, these are Family Walks and the grading should be read with this in mind. They apply to a fairly active six or seven year old, rather than a hardened veteran!

Easy Walks

Route 1 - *Westbury and the White Horse*
Route 2 - *Rode, Tellisford and the Somerset Frome*
Route 3 - *Lacock and Reybridge*
Route 5 - *Wellow and Stony Littleton Long Barrow*
Route 15 - *Moorend, Bury Hill and the Bristol Frome*
Route 16 - *Oldbury and the Severn*

Moderately difficult

Route 4 - *The Kennet and Avon Canal*
Route 7 - *Swineford and the Bristol Avon*
Route 8 - *Stanton Prior, Marksbury and Stantonbury Hill*
Route 13 - *Brean Down near Weston-super-Mare*
Route 14 - *Leigh Woods and the Avon Gorge*

More Strenuous

Route 6 - *Swainswick, Woolley and Langridge*
Route 9 - *Ubley, Blagdon and the Mendip Hills*
Route 10 - *Ebbor Gorge, Mendips*
Route 11 - *Cheddar and the Gorge*
Route 12 - *Burrington Combe and High Mendip*

BUS OPERATORS IN THE AREA

All the country bus services in the area are operated by Badgerline, the country fleet name of Bristol Omnibus. The Head Office is: Bristol Omnibus Company Ltd., Berkeley House, Lawrence Hill, Bristol, BS5 0DZ. Telephone: Bristol 9558211.

WET WEATHER ALTERNATIVES Completely or partly under cover.

The Bristol and Bath area has such a vast range of attractions that knowing where to begin, never mind finish, is an impossible task! The following represent some of the more well-known attractions. An excellent publication - Somerset and Avon Map and Guide of Places to Visit - contains a much more comprehensive list, and is available locally. Further details of each attraction can be obtained from:

Bath Tourist Information Centre, Abbey Churchyard. Telephone Bath 62831.
Bristol City Information Centre, Colston House, Colston Street. Telephone Bristol 9293891.

MUSEUMS AND ART GALLERIES

Axbridge, King John's Hunting Lodge. Merchant's House circa 1500. Open April to September.
Bath, Burrow's Toy Museum. York Street. Open daily.
Bath, Carriage Museum. Circus Mews. Open daily.
Bath, Costume Museum. Assembly Rooms. Open daily.
Bath, Postal Museum. Pulteney Street. Open daily.
Blaise Castle House Museum, near Clifton. 300 years of everyday life. Open Saturday to Wednesday.
Bristol, City Museum and Art Gallery. Queens Road. Open daily.
Bristol, Wesley's Chapel. The Horsefair. Open daily, excluding Wednesdays.
Cheddar, Gough's Cave Museum. Open Easter to September daily.
Claverton, American Museum. Open April to October daily.
Lacock, Fox Talbot Museum of Photography. Open March to October daily.
Street Shoe Museum. Open Easter to October daily.
Wells Museum. Open daily.
Weston, Waxworks, Regent Street. Open Spring to September daily.
Weston, Museum, Burlington Street. Open daily.
Wookey, Fairground Collection and Madame Tussauds Storeroom. Open daily.

HISTORIC BUILDINGS

Bath Pump Rooms and Roman Baths. Open daily.
Bath, Number 1 Royal Crescent. Open March to October.
Bristol, Georgian House, Great George Street. Open daily.
Bristol, Red Lodge, Park Row. Open daily.
Dyrham House and Grounds. Open April to October.
Lacock Abbey. Open April to November.
Longleat House. Open Easter to September.
Wells, Bishops Palace. Open Sunday to Thursday, Easter to October.
Also **Bath Abbey, Bristol Cathedral** and **Wells Cathedral.**

INDUSTRIAL INTEREST

Bath, Camden Works Museum, Julian Road. Open daily.

Bristol, SS Great Britain. Open daily.

Bristol, Industrial Museum, Princes Wharf. Open daily excluding Thursdays and Fridays.

Wookey Hole Paper Museum. Open daily.

Bitton Railway Centre. Open weekends as advertised locally.

Claverton Pump House. Open Sundays April to October.

Chewton Mendip, Cheese Dairy. Open daily.

WILDLIFE

Axbridge, Ambleside Water Gardens. Open Easter to October.

Brean Down, Tropical Bird Gardens. Open daily April to October.

Brokerswood, near Trowbridge. Woodland Museum and Park. Open daily.

Bristol Zoo. Open daily.

Longleat Safari Park. Open March to October.

Rode, Tropical Bird Gardens. Open daily.

CAVES

Cheddar Caves. Open daily.

Wookey Hole Caves. Open daily.

It is always sensible to confirm opening days and times prior to a trip out.

FUNGI IN THE AVON GORGE (Route 14)

THE FAMILY WALKS SERIES

Family Walks on Anglesey. Laurence Main	ISBN 0 907758 66 5
Family Walks in Berkshire & North Hampshire. Kathy Sharp	ISBN 0 907758 37 1
Family Walks around Bristol, Bath & the Mendips. Nigel Vile	ISBN 0 907758 19 3
Family Walks around Cardiff & the Valleys. Gordon Hindess	ISBN 0 907758 54 1
Family Walks in Cheshire. Chris Buckland	ISBN 0 907758 29 0
Family Walks in Cornwall. John Caswell	ISBN 0 907758 55 X
Family Walks in the Cotswolds. Gordon Ottewell	ISBN 0 907758 15 0
Family Walks in the Dark Peak. Norman Taylor	ISBN 0 907758 16 9
Family Walks in East Sussex. Sally & Clive Cutter	ISBN 0 907758 71 1
Family Walks on Exmoor & the Quantocks. John Caswell	ISBN 0 907758 46 0
Family Walks in Gower. Amanda Green	ISBN 0 907758 63 0
Family Walks in Hereford & Worcester. Gordon Ottewell	ISBN 0 907758 20 7
Family Walks on the Isle of Wight. Laurence Main	ISBN 0 907758 56 8
Family Walks in the Lake District. Barry McKay	ISBN 0 907758 40 1
Family Walks in Mendip, Avalon & Sedgemoor. Nigel Vile	ISBN 0 907758 41 X
Family Walks in Mid Wales. Laurence Main	ISBN 0 907758 27 4
Family Walks in the New Forest. Nigel Vile	ISBN 0 907758 60 6
Family Walks in the North Wales Borderlands. Gordon Emery	ISBN 0 907758 50 9
Family Walks in North West Kent. Clive Cutter	ISBN 0 907758 36 3
Family Walks in the North Yorkshire Dales. Howard Beck	ISBN 0 907758 52 5
Family Walks in Oxfordshire. Laurence Main	ISBN 0 907758 38 X
Family Walks in Pembrokeshire. Laurence Main	ISBN 0 907758 75 4
Family Walks in Snowdonia. Laurence Main	ISBN 0 907758 32 0
Family Walks in South Derbyshire. Gordon Ottewell	ISBN 0 907758 61 4
Family Walks around the South Downs. Nick Channer	ISBN 0 907758 73 8
Family Walks in South Gloucestershire. Gordon Ottewell	ISBN 0 907758 33 9
Family Walks in South Shropshire. Marian Newton	ISBN 0 907758 30 4
Family Walks in South Yorkshire. Norman Taylor	ISBN 0 907758 25 8
Family Walks in the Staffordshire Peak & Potteries. Les Lumsdon	ISBN 0 907758 34 7
Family Walks around Stratford & Banbury. Gordon Ottewell	ISBN 0 907758 49 5
Family Walks in Suffolk. C J Francis	ISBN 0 907758 64 9
Family Walks in Surrey. Norman Bonney	ISBN 0 907758 74 6
Family Walks around Swansea. Raymond Humphreys	ISBN 0 907758 62 2
Family Walks in the Teme Valley. Camilla Harrison	ISBN 0 907758 45 2
Family Walks in Three Peaks & Malham. Howard Beck	ISBN 0 907758 42 8
Family Walks in Warwickshire. Geoff Allen	ISBN 0 907758 53 3
Family Walks in the Weald of Kent & Sussex. Clive Cutter	ISBN 0 907758 51 7
Family Walks in West London. Caroline Bacon	ISBN 0 907758 72 X
Family Walks in West Yorkshire. Howard Beck	ISBN 0 907758 43 6
Family Walks in the White Peak. Norman Taylor	ISBN 0 907758 09 6
Family Walks in Wiltshire. Nigel Vile	ISBN 0 907758 21 5
Family Walks in the Wye Valley. Heather & John Hurley	ISBN 0 907758 26 6

The publishers welcome suggestions for further titles in this series; and will be pleased to consider manuscripts relating to Derbyshire from new or established authors.

Scarthin Books of Cromford, in the Peak District, are also leading second-hand and antiquarian booksellers, and are eager to purchase specialised material, both ancient and modern.

Contact Dr. D. J. Mitchell, 01629 823272